From a fle writer
to
Prof Cohen

With Compliments
& Best Wishes

Arjun
New Delhi
18 Jan 2012

REFLECTIONS OF AN AIR WARRIOR

Group Captain
Arjun Subramaniam

KNOWLEDGE WORLD

KW Publishers Pvt Ltd
New Delhi

KNOWLEDGE WORLD

A KW Publishers Book
www.kwpublishers.com

Published in India by

Kalpana Shukla
KW Publishers Pvt Ltd
5A/4A, Ansari Road, Daryaganj, New Delhi 110002
email: knowledgeworld@vsnl.net/online.kw@gmail.com

ISBN: 978-81-87966-72-2

Typeset by Black Innovation, New Delhi and Printed at Rajkamal Electric Press, New Delhi.

Dedicated to

No 30 Squadron IAF
'The Rhinos'

Contents

SECTION II: AIR POWER AND GEOPOLITICS

एयर चीफ मार्शल एफ एच मेजर
प वि से मे अ वि से मे शौ च वा मे ए डी सी
Air Chief Marshal F H Major
PVSM AVSM SC VM ADC

Tel : (011) Off : 23012517
Res : 23017300
Fax : 23018853
E-mail : airhouse@bol.net.in

INDIAN AIR FORCE
1932-2007

वायु सेना मुख्यालय
नई दिल्ली-110011
Air Headquarters
New Delhi - 110 011

FOREWORD

In the modern world, the Aerospace power of a country, both military and civil, reflects its national power. Its impact is akin to, but has perhaps exceeded that of maritime power, on the growth and well-being of a nation; and also on its status in the international order. Itś tremendously enhanced capabilities have made it enormously utilitarian and effective - it is an instrument of choice. Premised, as it is on high-technology, large funding and skilled people, nations better endowed in those respects, have the lead.

Aerospace power comprises the hardware, the people and the organisation with its processes and interfaces. Quite clearly, it is the people that are the principal element, for they determine the quality of hardware, as well as organisational strength. The people are sourced from the populace and if the people are air-minded, of scientific temper and tech-savvy, the organisation would have its start from a much higher level. We in India, do lack air-mindedness – that boyish wonder for flight and aeroplanes!

The Indian Air Force seeks the right kind of people. Ensuring the all-round growth of those with us, to give IAF that competitive edge, is another challenge. Awareness of aerospace power, leadership skills and an operational-cum-safety orientation are vital areas for development. Each of these areas are deeply impacted by the spread and dissemination of organisational wisdom, personal and collective experiences. We do lack in that area, for there are very few of us who care to share effectively, other than in the most informal settings and small closed groups. This reluctance allows our knowledge, failures and successes to be dissipated over time - consequently, each generation re-learns and repeats.

I am therefore very pleased that Gp Capt Subramaniam has been different from the average air warrior in this respect and has regularly 'put pen to paper' on professional issues. He has written a number of articles, essays and papers, that have been published in our professional - military and safety journals. His style is honest, direct and easy. This book is a collation of some of his best and relevant pieces and offers the reader an interesting and critical look at operations, safety and life in the IAF along with leadership issues and dilemmas. He has demonstrated through his writings, forthrightness and focus on overall improvement of the Service. One may not always agree with his opinions but debate is always a good idea.

Air Force officers and all aviation people would find the Book useful and I recommend it to all, who have an 'air mind'. I do hope this endeavour will encourage and stimulate others to come forward as well and share their experiences with candour.

Jai Hind!

AIR CHIEF MARSHAL
CHIEF OF THE AIR STAFF

12 Oct 07

Lt Gen BJ Gupta, VSM
Commandant

Defence Services Staff College
Wellington (Nilgiris)
Tamil Nadu - 643 231

FROM THE COMMANDANT'S DESK

1.   It gives me great pleasure to see one of my faculty members come out with a book that deals with not only myriad facets of life in the IAF, which in many ways reflects the lives of all of us in uniform, but also on issues related to our strategic environment. What is unique about the book is its direct personal style, emanating from first-hand experiences of command, training and peace-time leadership.

2.   War fighting in the 21st century is going to be a complex affair with unconventional adversaries resorting to unpredictable tactics and strategies. In such a scenario, it is imperative for our officers to develop a probing mind, keen intellect, flexibility of thought, and courage of conviction in order to continuously challenge existing tactics, doctrine and concepts, something that is so very important to cope with the rapidly changing environment. The Defence Services Staff College is an ideal place to amalgamate academic excellence with operational experience, and translate it into tactics, strategy and doctrine. We need to upgrade our focus and I would like to urge other members of the faculty to share their rich experiences with both the next generation, and the present leadership.

(BJ Gupta)
Lieutenant General
Commandant
20 Sep 07

Acknowledgements

I have had the privilege of serving under some fine Commanding Officers over the years and I would like to place on record my gratitude to them for shaping my attitudes-little did they know that I had this dirty habit of scribbling my impressions of what they did or did not do and store it for posterity! I am also grateful to my rather 'strict' instructor AVM Yajurvedi for encouraging me to write when he was the DFS, to Air Cmde Jasjit Singh for stoking the fire further and asking me to 'keep at it' whenever we interacted, to AVM Kalia, my Chief Instructor at DSSC Wellington for encouraging intellectual growth and giving me the space to put together this book, and to my publishers, Knowledge World, for supporting this fledgling attempt of mine. I am deeply indebted to Lt Gen B J Gupta, Commandant DSSC for adding value to the book. The Chief of Air Staff, Air Chief Marshal F H Major has been most magnanimous to pen the foreword to this book; I am sure this will inspire others to put pen to paper more often.

The views expressed in the book are those of the author and do not in any way reflect the views of the IAF or Government of India.

FLIGHT SAFETY AND LEADERSHIP SECTION

FLIGHT SAFETY HAS TO BE A WAY OF LIFE. IT IS NON NEGOTIABLE AND EVERY AIR WARRIOR HAS TO IMBIBE THE ESSENTIALS OF THE OPERATIONAL, MAINTENANCE AND HUMAN ASPECTS OF FLIGHT SAFETY IF WE ARE TO BUILD A SUSTAINABLE AIR FORCE OF THE FUTURE.

LEARN TO LEAD, LEAD TO FIGHT AND FIGHT TO WIN

INSCRIPTION AT TACDE, THE IAF'S TACTICS AND
COMBAT DEVELOPMENT ESTABLISHMENT

IN THE HOT SEAT — THE OPENING SHOT

*T*his series of articles, with emphasis on leadership and flight safety, was
*published over a period of three issues in the Flight Safety Magazine of the IAF
in 2002 after the author completed a successful command of a fighter squadron —*

an assignment every fighter pilot worth his salt dreams of. The articles were commended by Air Chief Marshal Latif, a retired Chief of Air Staff (CAS). A copy of that letter is placed at the end of this section. They also evoked tremendous response across the rank and file of the IAF, a fact that is corroborated by an email from the Editor of Flight Safety Magazine that was sent to the author while he was on deputation abroad (certainly not an exercise in blowing his own trumpet). The articles were also included by the Directorate of Air Staff Inspection for their Handbook for Flight Commanders.

The Opening Shot

Command of a squadron, be it a fighter, helicopter, transport, missile or radar squadron, is probably a period of reckoning and transition for any professional in the IAF. Over the years, I have had the privilege of serving under a number of distinguished Commanding Officers, each one of them leaving lasting impressions on me of what was right and wrong. I stored these as jottings for posterity, hoping that I could learn from them and not forget things in a hurry. As the years went by, I saw squadrons perform brilliantly under one Commanding Officer (CO) and slip into mediocrity under the next. Why this was happening was very puzzling initially, but as I grew in service, the mystery unravelled. Leadership styles were so personality oriented that units swayed to the Samba beat of the CO. There was very little feedback from the outgoing CO to the new guy; probably an attitude of "I have done my bit, now it is for you to find your feet and then let us see how you do compared to me". This led to most COs having to reinvent the wheel, though I was lucky that I was briefed thoroughly on taking over; an exception rather than the rule, I guess.

By now, it had dawned on me that most squadrons ran on the personality of the CO. This to me is an archaic and rather regressive trend as fighting units should be able to function despite the personality of the CO, which, at times, could be flawed. Since most COs have to literally start from scratch, I wondered where institutional building would start and why our service was so personality oriented at all levels, unlike some other air forces. It is extremely important that successes and follies, even during peacetime, need to be recorded and handed over for posterity. Opinions, projects visualised but never executed, recurring problem areas, and many more — all need to be documented honestly and left behind. Fear not the ridicule or contempt that your failures will elicit, but rejoice when you hear that they have never been repeated — that is what institution building is all about. Most, or all of what *I WOULD LIKE TO SHARE*, has been articulated by many COs from time to

time; what I have only tried to do with all humility is transfer old wine from a casket into a packaged bottle.

I would have loved to include a number of operational aspects of command, but I felt that this was not a weak area in our air force. Rather, I felt that leadership issues, man/resource management and conflict management need to be addressed honestly at lower levels of leadership by someone who has been part of that group. Let this, your first command, be a fruitful one as mine has been and may you REACH FOR THE SKY WITH PRIDE AND ELAN. I would be failing in my duty if I did not thank the Rhinos for making this possible, and Fg Offrs Bhatnagar, Banerjee, Nautiyal and the cartoonist at the Directorate of Flight Safety for livening things up with their cartoons, albeit to the dismay of my wife, who wished that they had added a few strands to my bald pate.

KEY RESULT AREAS

Key result areas (KRAs) seems to be a very familiar and pet topic of senior commanders; however, at lower field formations, KRAs seem to have lost their meaning in mundane day-to-day operations. Does it happen, and why does it happen? KRAs are meant to provide focus to a commander and enable him to lay down priorities based on directions from higher formations. Absence or non adherence to KRAs leads to short-term targets dictated mainly by the demands of your immediate boss and stunts your own ability to dictate the pace of work in your unit. This is not to say that the KRAs of your Air Officer Commanding/Station Commander will not be in overall conformity with that of the IAF. It is just that there is greater satisfaction in laying down your own KRAs based on your resources, the capability of your team and ground realities, which at times are ignored by higher formations.

So, lay down an achievable set of KRAs and delegate responsibility to core groups — hic! I can see many squadron commanders saying "Hey! Look at him talking through his hat, here I don't have crew to man ORPs or combat teams and he is talking about core groups to execute KRAs". So, you have to head each core group, scale down your expectations from your team, yet lay down goals and targets, or you run the danger of drifting aimlessly downstream for two years. Rest assured that a tremendous sense of achievement will permeate through the unit on reaching even small targets. Don't be vague about your KRAs and leave them as Professional Excellence, Op Preparedness, etc. Be more specific in each domain, as shown in Table 1.1.

Table 1.1 Key Result Areas

PROFESSIONAL EXCELLENCE	OP PREPAREDNESS	MORALE
Quality training	Proficiency in air combat	Team building
Safe flying environment	Proficiency in combat interceptions	Team spirit
Technology orientation	Search and Rescue (SAR) capability	Welfare

More often than not, the fear of failure prevents us from laying down specific targets. Remember, it is better to have tried your best and failed rather than not to have tried at all. So! If your KRAs have remained unchanged for the last 10 years, brush the cobwebs off and have the vision to change them for a set of reasonable, achievable and sensible KRAs.

LET YOUR JUNIORS GROW

It was shift changeover time on the tarmac one afternoon, and I had to address all the Engineering Officers, Warranted ranks and Sergeants on a sensitive issue. We gathered in the cafeteria, little realising that two aircraft were still flying and would be taxiing in any moment. And sure enough, they did. There was no desk i/c and tarmac leader, both Warrant Officers sprang up, but I told them to sit down and quietly went outside. For a few seconds there was confusion but the recovery was heart-warming. The senior-most Corporal around donned the tarmac leader's jacket, another assumed the lead marshaller's role and the rest fell in place. No big deal! On the face of it — yes! But I was happy because it validated my belief that if you let juniors grow, give them responsibility with accountability and let them make mistakes with immediate corrective inputs, they will rise to the occasion whenever the need came up. Like the dominating Banyan tree that provides shade and comfort but allows very little to grow beneath its intimidating branches, many commanding officers believe that as long as they *deliver*, very little else matters. One of the casualties of this approach is the development of your team. Why does this happen? Many senior commanders have, in their addresses, briefings and informal interactions in the field lamented on this malaise. Yet, translating these into progressive action has been painfully slow. There are a number of reasons why subordinates are not allowed to grow and it is important to honestly assess whether you belong to the 'I' or 'we' category before going further. Only if you belong to the latter should you read on. What are the *symptoms* of a unit in which the decision-making process is highly centralised?

- No/very few decisions are taken by the Flight Commander, Senior Technical Officer or the Adjutant.
- There is a visible lack of confidence amongst junior officers, even though the squadron may be doing very well.
- Very few brainstorming sessions are conducted and even if they are, they are generally monologues by the CO.
- Though everything may be ok within the unit—or at least so it may seem, there is a simmering discontentment, which can only be discerned by an outsider.
- Dissent or differences in opinion regarding tactics, administration or maintenance practices is frowned upon, even if it is well meant and directed at the overall improvement of the air force.

What is at the root of this environment? Is it solely because of the CO's personality, or because of the environment and work culture, or a combination of both? To be very fair to all my contemporaries and predecessors, it is a combination of the man and his environment. Reasons for our inability, albeit at times to nurture our subordinates — be it the Flight Commander, or the Squadron Warrant Officer — are manifold. A few of these are enumerated below, which, I hope will generate a lot of heat and indignation amongst the numerous COs who take pride in team building, as also provoke some *soul searching amongst those who hold the reigns too tightly.*

- *Fear of failure:* This is, by far, the most common reason for not delegating adequately. A lot in our air force goes by reputation, and it is this reputation that is guarded at all cost.
- Next is an environmental malaise, commonly known as *'Zero Error Syndrome'*. However hard we may try, it raises its ugly head from time to time and, coupled with the fear of failure, you have a potent mix. I am reminded of an attempt not so very long ago to replace this *Zero Error Syndrome* with a *No Compromise Syndrome*; a very laudable attempt at ushering in responsibility and accountability. Sadly, the attempt was half hearted and did not take off.
- *Sense of personal inadequacy and insecurity:* Many a time this character trait proves decisive in stunting the growth of subordinates. Lack of faith in one's own ability leads to a reluctance in exploiting others' strengths, little realising that the sum total will never add up favourably. At times there is also the fear of being upstaged by a competent and professionally sound subordinate. Very few of us are good at everything and as a CO you are no different. Since the air force has found you fit to *command,* be honest to yourself, work to your strengths and don't hide your personal weaknesses. If you have a good back-up within the unit, use it. Remember that *it is your team that is performing and not you individually.* If, in the bargain, one of your subordinates hogs the limelight, have the magnanimity to step back and let him *enjoy his moment of glory;* that is what maturity is all about.
- *Inadequate Organisational Support:* Military decision making, by nature, has been highly centralised down the ages, primarily due to *human life being involved.* It is only in recent times that the advent of technology coupled with an explosion in HRD techniques has forced men in uniform to critically examine the aspect of optimum exploitation of manpower. The exuberance and flexibility of youth may convince a *'hitting forty'* CO of the need to delegate, but a battle-hardened *'fifty plus'* veteran, who has not delegated

earlier, will find it extremely difficult as the AOC/Station Commander to do so suddenly. Unless the establishment and the organisation exhort him to imbibe the *mantra of delegation and decentralisation*, it is not fair to expect him to do so.

This is what Gen Chuck Horner, the distinguished Air force Commander during Desert Storm had to say about delegation and decentralisation in his book *Every Man A Tiger* — *"If you impose excessive control to bring about order, then you will snuff initiative. My job was to exploit professionals and get them to produce their best. I had to focus them and then let them be themselves. Sometimes this generated friction, conflicts or even explosions. So be it. A little friction is the price you pay for getting everyone to act and to use their initiative and talents; and this was especially true of the high spirited people I was usually lucky enough to command."*

What then needs to be done to ensure that you allow your subordinates to grow? *You are the key!* Don't lament about a hostile environment or lack of organisational support. Nor should you ride piggyback on your immediate boss and palm off your inability to delegate on him! Start with small things, and as you find them succeeding, you will move on to larger key issues. The key to successful delegation is your ability to:

- Lay down broadly what you want with targets
- Monitor progress continuously and insist on feedback
- Intervene at critical moments
- Allow mistakes to take place, as long as they do not jeopardise flight safety, morale and financial propriety
- Appreciate a job well done and censure shoddy work
- Look at the *big picture when it comes to assessments*

Some of the random issues that accelerated subordinate development in our unit are enumerated below. They are squadron specific and could vary according to different environments and capability of subordinates:

- Allow the flight commander to run the *show*, whether it comes to flying operations, leave planning or raising uninfluenced Annual Reports, but be there to help him in an invisible manner.
- Integrate the Engineering Officers into all squadron activity. You have to give them responsibility in areas totally divorced from maintenance in order to make them feel part of the unit. This, apart from contributing to the progress of the unit, will develop them into versatile and confident officers.

- Offer opinions regularly, but ensure that you make it appear as unobtrusive as possible. Let your stamp not dilute the satisfaction of doing things correctly.
- There is a lot of talent amongst young officers but it takes a while to get them to shrug off their reticence and display their individual prowess. You have to cajole and motivate them at times; it is worth the effort.
- Warrant ranks hold the key to efficient administration of matters relating to your men. ***Responsibility with accountability*** should be the mantra for their development. As the officer community, we have spoon-fed our warrant ranks for too long now and they seek to be directed at every step rather than lead.

If we want to develop our juniors, the maxim ***no pain no gain*** has to be accepted. The pain I am referring to has to be borne by us, the commanding officers. There will be many times when you are summoned to the *sanctum* of the AOC/Stn Cdr and given a dressing down because of slip-ups by members of your team. Take it in your stride and soak up the indictment as long as you know that the slip-up was a result of lack of experience or an oversight. Lash out immediately and you run the risk of your subordinates saying 'next time, I take no decision; let Winco bell the cat'. There goes your honourable intent of decentralising the decision-making process. One could go on and on but I guess the point is driven home. The process of decentralising is a slow and painful process all over, made even more difficult in areas that deal with human life and expensive equipment. That it is inescapable is also becoming clearer in an age where multi-skilling is being increasingly talked about as a necessity to tackle the *resource crunch*. If you have it in you to delegate, nurture and absorb flak, then you are *a twenty-first century commander.* I say *go for it,* the air force of tomorrow will benefit.

It would be appropriate to wind up this chapter with a live anecdote. Exasperated with me over a trivial issue, THE BOSS dismissed me with a wave and said, " Subbu, why don't you push off on leave; the squadron runs so much better when you are not around". I am sure he did not mean it as a compliment, but it was music to my ears as it reflected the calibre of my team. It is another story, however, why I could not go on leave!

GETTING ALONG WITH THE BOSS

Notwithstanding who the boss is at home, you have no choice in the matter at work. So partner! The odds are heavily stacked against you in this power struggle. Have no illusions and you will be a happy and contented soul; harbour any grandiose plan for dominance and you have a readymade script for a pot-

boiler of a soap opera. Ok! Jokes apart, it is very important for a Squadron Commander/CO to foster and maintain a healthy working relationship with the AOC/Stn Cdr; a relationship that is based on mutual professional respect, faith, and social cordiality rather than subservience or sycophancy, colloquially called in Hinglish the 'jee sir mentality'. For this you have to be a good judge of human character, moods and idiosyncrasies and use them for the overall good of the unit, and indirectly, the air force. It is always good to start your tenure with a letter to the AOC/Stn Cdr expressing your willingness to work as part of his *team*, of which your unit is an integral part. Be quietly confident and observant in the beginning rather than starting off aggressively in your interaction with him. Make your point and stick to your guns; but do so with dignity and restraint. How does one categorise *bosses?* Simple! There are the easy to get along with types and difficult customers. Pray that you draw the first one but be prepared for the second variety too because it takes all types to make this glorious air force of ours. Being a little more specific and yet avoiding any high-flown management jargon, be prepared for the following types :

- Advisor
- Facilitator and Team Builder
- Authoritarian Dictator
- Benevolent Dictator

The first two types are easy to handle and get along with as they lay down achievable targets and allow you to do your job your own way, but within a wide canvass of how they think things *ought to be*. Delegation, team building, a *no-nonsense and no frills approach* are their trademarks. How do you identify this genre? They are:

- Quietly confident
- Good listeners
- Principled but not rigid
- Empathetic and friendly, with a disarming personality that puts people at ease
- Not given to taking spontaneous and immediate decisions
- Capable of switching off and on quickly
- Able to remain fairly composed under stress.

Treat them with respect and value their judgement/advice and you will have the freedom to *breathe, lead and command.* For this category, the means are as

ADVISOR   TEAM BUILDER   DICTATOR

important as the end. On the flip side, don't take them for granted and let there not be a breach of trust in any form, or else you run the risk of quietly being ignored and left out of the decision-making loop; something that will hurt you and your unit. Honesty and integrity are numero uno in their list of priorities and they display them without flaunting the 'I am ok and you are not' veneer. Needless to say, a rare breed; often misunderstood by the establishment as being *soft*. The most common *bosses* you will encounter belong to the dictatorial cadre! Believe me when I say that they are not too difficult to cope with; they just need to be handled like glass, i.e. with care. They are normally high achievers, pushy, sharp and highly rigid about the *rightness* of their agenda for the station. Empathy, constructive feedback and meaningful discussions are alien to them, and, 'in my time' a favourite cliché. How you tackle them depends entirely on your personality. If you too are a type A personality, i.e. aggressive, impatient and highly result oriented, you would hit it off well with the boss as long as you don't clash with him in public and contradict him frequently, something that you will find very hard to do, because of your inherent personality. If there is a conflict it is bound to be a David vs Goliath clash, the only difference being that Goliath will be the victor. So don't bank on the Bible to bale you out; gracefully back off after having put your point across. If you are a *quiet achiever,* life would be much easier when it comes to dealing with a 'hyper boss'. Your calm and cool temperament may serve as an ideal foil to his, and who knows! In times of hectic activity and stress, you could provide a calming touch. The only danger you face is of being steamrolled frequently. The answer to this is to lay down your own threshold of tolerance keeping, in mind the honour and sanctity of the post you occupy. The bottom line in any relationship ought to be *air force, unit, men, the officers you command, and lastly, yourself.*

PACE YOURSELF

Yes! The adrenalin must be flowing when you take over command of a squadron. Pause a while and take stock of what your predecessor has left behind. If the squadron has done well under his command, you need to reflect as to how to build on his solid innings rather than embarking on an ego-intensive 'doing things my way only'. The former approach will allow you to observe, assess, and fine-tune the existing operational, maintenance and admin environment in the squadron. It will form part of the *consolidation* phase for you as a professional and the unit as a whole. Team building and concentration on KRAs will prevent unnecessary wastage of energy, thereby allowing you to dictate the pace of continuity or *change*, as well as when you want the pace stepped up.

Having established your own credentials, proved yourself as a professional and built a team, you can now embark on your agenda for the squadron. Over the years you would have tucked away small memories of various aspects of the diaspora of the air force way of life; with the hope of implementing some of it and discarding some. This is your first opportunity in service to do so; do so with care and remember that it takes years to build traditions. Do not try to do too many things in this *consolidation phase* of your command, or you run the risk of doing very little that will stand the test of time. Identify your strengths, draw up plans and execute them systematically with one aim in mind, viz. progress of the squadron, the station and the IAF. Do not seek any personal glory; personal satisfaction — yes! Very often has a squadron slipped because of misplaced personal ambition.

All this while, do not lose focus on operations, flight safety and training. If operations are your forte, concentrate on them; provided you have a good team to back you up in admin and training. Similarly, if admin/man management is your strength, have the courage to allow your operationally strong flight commander to implement your plans and take charge of the day-to-day operations. In no way does this mean that you have abdicated responsibility in that area; you are just exploiting your team's *strengths* to the hilt. Remember, all your attempts to spruce up the unit, introduce welfare measures and consolidate finances will come to nought if you slip up on operations and flight safety.

Having completed the *consolidation*, it is time to tackle problem areas so that you leave the unit in good shape for your successor. So, if you have had the fortune of taking over a unit in fine shape, for heaven's sake leave it in the same or better condition.

- Do not fritter away your predecessor's good work—the very least you can maintain is status quo.
- In such a situation, be ambitious, be a high achiever, think not of yourself, but of the unit; you can't go wrong.

If you have had the misfortune of taking over an outfit in the dumps, it is a different ball-game altogether. The buzzword then has to be clinical change. There is no time for consolidation or taking stock. You have to stem the rot, make sweeping changes and take hard decisions, something that we shall discuss later. Very rarely will you find a squadron that is operationally strong but administratively weak; however, it is quite likely that you may find a unit that is administratively strong but operationally weak.

The worst situation is one in which a squadron is both operationally and administratively in the doldrums. The latter is a tough call and you have to act swiftly and decisively. Having stemmed the rot, pause a while and take a breather; let your team acknowledge that your moves have paid dividend. This is consolidation time for you too, to rest before picking up steam. Leave, picnics, early pack-ups and get-togethers are good ways of giving your team a break. All this while, do not forget yourself! Keep yourself fit, active and healthy. Spend quality time with your family and friends and don't appear as though the worries of the whole world have descended on your shoulders. Take adequate leave; it is important to recharge your own batteries periodically. Remind yourself constantly of an age-old prayer that invokes the qualities of moral courage, restraint and maturity and goes like this, "God give me the strength to change the things I can, the equanimity to accept the things I can't and the wisdom to differentiate between the two". Frustration, fear and excessive ambition will drain you, while hope, vigour and a positive attitude will see you through, so that when you hand over command, you do so with a sense of achievement and pride.

TACKLING A DILEMMA—OP PREPAREDNESS OR FLIGHT SAFETY

Before discussing this issue at length, it would be appropriate to ponder over the excerpts of a letter written in 1985 to all aircrew in Central Air Command by the then Air Officer Commanding-in-Chief, Air Marshal J W Greene, PVSM, AVSM, Vr C.

In peacetime we fly mostly to train for war. In addition, the transport, helicopter and certain other units have their special or routine tasks, which are dovetailed with training. I would like to share my thoughts with you on priorities and responsibilities associated with peacetime flying.

In peacetime, when there is no requirement to "do or die", your first priority is to return the aircraft to the inventory holder without damage or without having exceeded any limitations of the airframe, engine and systems. You may like to ponder on the connotations of this brief statement and fully understand them. It means that you as a pilot must:

- Be fully satisfied that the aircraft is not only serviceable at the time you signed for it but also that the aircraft has been maintained and cared for in a manner which will ensure that it remains fully serviceable while in your custody. To ensure this, you will have to associate yourself with various maintenance activities. You must let it be known that you care for the men who maintain your machine or equipment and appreciate their effort.

- Be confident that you have the ability to handle the aircraft or equipment under all possible conditions. Here you must consider your own physiological and psychological states to be sure that you can cope. This is an individual responsibility that cannot be compromised.

- Be fully aware of the strengths and weaknesses of the environment, such as performance and reliability of avionics, navigation and recovery aids, controllers, radars, supporting services, etc. If you want to guarantee the safe return of your aircraft and operability of critical sensors at critical times, you must be sure not only of yourself, but also that nothing you depend on will let you down. If you let it be known that **you depend on these sensors or systems and the people who maintain them, the men in charge are bound to do their best to support you.** Here again, you must appreciate the support rendered and quality of services provided.

- Be fully aware of your own strengths and weaknesses so that clear lines can be drawn as to how far you can go. Many of us are unwilling to come to terms with ourselves and we generally avoid such self-appraisal. Consequently, we tend to press on regardless, deep into grey areas.

There should be no doubt in the minds of COs — whether they are commanding operational flying, Surface-to-Air Guided Weapons or Radar squadrons — that op preparedness remains numero uno in their list of priorities. However, modern ac, equipment and aircrew are so valuable that an air force like ours needs to preserve them for a rainy day too. This is where flight safety comes in; putting it rather simply, it is all about **saving and preserving vital assets.** So, how does one go about ensuring a work ethos wherein operational preparedness and flight safety complement rather than conflict with each other? There exists a certain dichotomy between the two in the IAF, and to unravel this mystery it is important to list the important ingredients of both facets, identify conflicting requirements and work out a suitable reconciliation plan. The following list identifies certain behavioural aspects associated with both op preparedness and flight safety, but with different connotations. It is by no means comprehensive and totally representative and has the flexibility to adapt to various environments.

OP PREPAREDNESS	FLIGHT SAFETY
Aggressiveness	Caution
Risk-taking ability	Circumspection
Confidence	Overconfidence
Initiative	Supervision
Need to push	Caution
Leadership	Leadership
Stress management	Stress management
Team spirit	Team spirit
Decision making	Decision making

You as the CO have your task clearly cut out for solving dichotomies where they exist, and going one step further, by stressing that there is no choice in the matter when it comes to the co-existence of op preparedness and flight safety. It is your job to temper aggression with caution, draw a line between confidence and overconfidence, instill honesty amongst your team to equate risk-taking propensity with intrinsic ability, and decide when to push, how much to push, whom to push and when to stop before fatigue results in a blunder. Leadership, team spirit and decision making are vital for both; don't for a moment equate them only with op preparedness. Excessive caution stunts op preparedness whilst a gung-ho approach, throwing caution to the wind many a time results in a flight safety aberration. In short, drawing the line somewhere in between, depending on the capability of your team, is how you will achieve the right balance. Tremendous maturity is what is needed to ensure that both co-exist. Do you have it in you?

CONFLICT MANAGEMENT

Whenever groups of people interact, there is bound to be conflict. In earlier days, conflict management in the air force was a fairly easy task, with the CO having to intervene only in extreme circumstances. Officers were highly motivated and focused; men were hardy and proud of donning the air force blue; ladies content to enjoy life on an air force camp, proud to be married into the services and mentally prepared to face the trials and tribulations of life in a growing organisation.

Things are quite different today; almost half your time as a CO is spent in conflict management of various kinds. An equal amount of time is also likely to be spent in convincing your old man *(who would invariably belong to the old school)* that conflict exists in various forms — be it inter-branch turf battles, interpersonal conflict or environment-related conflicts — all of which severely eat into precious time, which otherwise could have been devoted to operations and training. This is something that is here to stay and needs your constant attention. Conflict in squadrons is of two kinds; professional and social. While the former is easy to resolve, the latter can be quite time consuming and frustrating. Professional conflict could relate to any of the aspects mentioned below. There are no quick fix and ready-made solutions for them. In fact, they demand a fair degree of flexibility and ingenuity to resolve and depend on too many variables, much like the weather. The bottom line while resolving these conflicts is fairness, firmness and keeping service interests above personal interests. Some of the most common conflicts relate to:

- Methods of achieving various tasks
- Inter-branch turf battles
- Conduct of flying operations — my way or your way! This could be between the CO and the Flt Cdr, or between the CO and the AOC
- Role and contribution of the support services
- Priority given to general service training, like PT, Parade, Boards of officers and Courts of Inquiries
- Achievement of task vis-à-vis flight safety and crew fatigue

Some of the more common social conflicts that have the potential to affect the working relationships within a unit are:

- Officers' social contribution/obligations vis-à-vis family commitments
- Ego clashes between ladies caused by varying backgrounds, educational qualifications and the different ways in which they look at their role in making the unit a congenial place for their husbands to work in.
- Conduct of social functions

Ladies have a very important role in minimizing conflict within a unit; however, ladies married into the services today are generally confused about the role they play, not in furthering their husbands' careers, but in helping them do their best! I hope the subtle difference is noted. Why is there a general unwillingness to contribute wholeheartedly in any unit endeavour? Why is any social contribution seen as a bind? One has only to look at the opportunities in Civvy Street for ladies to zero in onto the problem. Having interacted with a wide cross-section of ladies, one feels that their individual aspirations are at times stifled, and they are unwilling to look at their role as *homemakers* in the air force with pride. This is where the CO's wife has the onerous responsibility of motivating, educating and helping ladies feel proud of having married into the air force. Therein alone lies the solution that many units face. Let us face it, conflict is inevitable; what is in our hands is the speed and manner in which we can resolve conflict. Working in perfect harmony or *sync* is a dream—conflict resolution is the key to this treasure; try to find it.

AIR FORCE WIVES' PRAYER

Dear Lord
Give me the greatness of heart to see
The difference between duty and his love for me.
Give me the understanding so that I may know
When duty calls him, he must go.
Give me a task each day
To fill the time he's away.
Oh Lord, when he must fly so high
Watch over him and keep him nigh.
When he is in a foreign land
Keep him safe in your loving hand.
And Lord, when the deployment is so long
Please stay with me and keep me strong.
AMEN.
(This is something that I inserted into the book at the last moment because it
rang so true.I hope you feel so too!)

(Columbus Air Force Base, Mississippi, US of A)

FEEDBACK AND PERFORMANCE COUNSELLING

Feedback and performance counselling are vital HR tools for commanders to feel the pulse of their units. The dilemma facing many a CO is whether to create an atmosphere of 'glasnost', wherein feedback is readily available and forthcoming, or to stick to traditional military channels of communication in which feedback is *filtered* all the way up, losing its sting en route. The advantages of the former are that it conforms to present trends all over the world that encourage transparency as a powerful tool to improve a system. On the flip side, it may result in a laissez faire attitude creeping in and leading, at times, to a breakdown of discipline. It may also result in the CO's having to spend far too much time listening to complaints, inputs and suggestions rather than doing something. The latter option is a time-tested, conservative and safe one, in which feedback and suggestions are frowned at, but nevertheless accepted as a *routine log it affair.* Any resultant suggestions upwards from you are routine, non-controversial, and follow the "Don't rock the boat" style of leadership. To be very frank, the first option is risky and frustrating, but with greater reward and satisfaction, if successful, you could have provided a catalyst for a long-desired change.

Performance counselling of officers is another grey area where COs prefer to stay away from conflict with their subordinates and use the pen to good effect while filling Annual Reports. While it is easy to recognize and reward the high achievers and censure the absolute non-performers, it is the moderate achiever who suffers the maximum because of the absence of honest and direct counselling from time to time. How many times have we seen a youngster shake his head in disbelief after having received his first performance feedback from Air HQ, which tells him that he is a mediocre performer? More often than not, the poor blighter would not have been apprised of his mediocre performance because by the book his performance has been satisfactory, i.e. 5 and 6 and the IO/RO would have conveniently avoided any meaningful counselling. As CO, you owe it to the organization, your subordinates and yourself, to apprise your subordinates of their actual performance. Too often have we seen COs who avoid *critical* counselling as they see it as a source of conflict, fearing that negative feedback will lead to *switching off* rather than improvement. This leads to a rationalisation of accepting mediocrity, as most operational units are perpetually short of operational crew. The CO is in a dilemma whether to crack the whip on mediocrity and overload the high performers or keep everyone superficially happy and extract whatever he can from the *mediocres*. It is a Hobson's choice. You could be transparent, blunt and adopt a no-nonsense hacking approach, and risk your mediocre guys becoming non-performers. Experience shows that positive strokes and genuine attempts to improve the average performers work better than wielding the whip. Or, you could be a goody guy; avoid calling a spade a spade and conducting honest AR debriefs; avoid any conflict and don't waste time working on your average guys. The attitude being — *let them fall by the wayside, it is their own doing.* This is a typical attitude that gains favour at times because of the pressures on a CO to deliver, due to which he worries about the end result and not the means. In this scenario, a few good men shoulder the entire responsibility, thereby relegating teamwork to the background. What is the way out of this quagmire? One thing is certain — we cannot afford to let trained professionals get de-motivated in the prime of their career; and who are the guys responsible? It is you! Commanding Officers of field formations, on whom this onerous responsibility lies. You will be faced with a number of conflicting inputs, some from the top and others from the bottom— some that say *do not accept anything but the best* and others that say *this is what is available. Make do with it.* Some will say, *one rotten apple spoils the basket — throw it out,* while ground reality states that throwing the rotten apple out only means taxing your shining ones more, since the establishment cannot replace

the apple in a hurry. In my opinion, the single biggest challenge facing medium-level commanders is not an operational one or a logistics problem; it is an HR problem of how to keep your average performers motivated and contribute effectively to the overall performance of the unit. Some principles, which yielded rich dividend during my tenure as a CO, in an environment that was marked by a perpetual material and human resource crunch, are enumerated below:

- Positive strokes yield better results than wielding the whip.
- Average performers are generally given a feeling that they are not wanted, and this results in alienation—make them feel wanted and exploit their strengths.
- Be patient — don't dish out warnings like peanuts.
- Lay down your threshold of tolerance, one which everyone clearly understands.
- AR debriefs need to be as transparent as can be — do not let an average performer get away with a feeling that he has done well. However, learn to coat your debrief with words of encouragement rather than giving a ring of finality to your verdict by saying "you are not living up to your potential — what is bothering you? You have it in you, and yet …?"
- Do understand that the *best may not be joining us* — we have to make them the best of them, which demands skill, tact, vision and leadership skills of the highest order. So assume your role as juggler and balance the requirements of the service, which has to say that it accepts nothing but the best, and what you actually have is somewhere in between.

HAPPY COUNSELLING!

RANDOM MUSINGS

Calculated risk!

Hard decision!

ON TAKING CALCULATED RISKS

There are times when you have to be prepared to take risks, not foolish risks but calculated ones. For this you have to first understand the concept of risk taking in very simple terms which is dependent on the following variables in a squadron-level context:

- Your personality
- Your commander's personality
- Environmental compulsions
- Organizational compulsions
- Related pay-offs.

Why does one need to take a risk during peacetime operations? This is a question that many will ask. Many will also question the need to take any administrative risks since the organization is supposed to cater to all kinds of contingencies and the needs of field units. At times, an agency or authority that is supposed to take an executive decision, fails to do so for various reasons, indecisiveness and procrastination being the most common ones. This leaves field units with two options. The first is a passive *waiting game* in which *red tapism and bureaucratic procedures* have a field day, with files moving furiously till a decision is finally taken, after exhausting the unit. The second option is to force a decision by taking a risk and hoping that it gets vindicated. This is as far as financial and administrative risks are concerned. But, what of flying-related risks? Here, do tread with utmost caution and break down your risk taking into clearly defined compartments. These compartments conform more or less to the *restrictions laid down in various orders for flying and operations.* This is how they look.

Under-Training (U/T) Flying: No chances should be taken at all except for giving them an experience of flying in marginal weather conditions in trainer aircraft. If you have a doubt, don't launch and trust your judgment or that of your senior supervisors. The payoff of safety is tremendous, though you would be accused, albeit rarely, that you are mollycoddling your youngsters. Your retort should ring loud and clear — that the youngsters have a whole lifetime of flying for the pace to be upped.

Fully Operational Training: Calculated risks within the framework of existing rules can be taken after gauging the capability of the individual, state of the flying environment and prevailing philosophy, with regard to operations at higher formations. An examples of this is the various directives that are issued from time to time related to Dissimilar Air Combat Training with other types of aircraft, integrated exercises and conduct of major command-level exercises. It must be remembered that *these so-called risks are actually vital tools to help the leadership gauge the actual operational capability of the forces they command.* Launch and recovery of missions in stringent and often marginal weather conditions and waiver of the fatigue limit of four sorties a day after due consideration by the appropriate authority are some common risks that squadrons take from time to time. Just remember that there is a time and place to take calculated risks, and, as far as possible keep your AOC/Stn Cdr apprised of any risks you want to take. Payoffs here too are important; do stick to the maxim of low risk and maximum payoff as against a high-risk, ego-driven approach to risk taking, where the payoffs are minimal.

ON TOLERATING MEDIOCRITY

At times it is impossible, for reasons of expediency, to weed out incompetent officers. The establishment may not accept this, but realities in the field do compel commanders into accepting mediocrity at times. Hang on! I am not for one moment condoning this approach; all I am trying to do is to brainstorm my way around the problem. Instead of cursing the establishment for saddling you with mediocre guys and then procrastinating when it comes to taking action against incompetence, why don't you try to exploit their strengths and devise means to reduce the effect of their negative traits on the unit? Every CO has to lay down a threshold of tolerating incompetence and not hesitate to take drastic remedial action in case this threshold is crossed. Tackling mediocrity with an iron fist often results in the high performers being saddled with extra work for too long; something that is detrimental in the long run. This happens because the establishment takes too long to provide replacements, an oft-repeated 'make do with what you have' is what normally flows down.

In small units, one has, at times to, tolerate mediocrity for the sake of harmony. There is also a tendency to over-assess mediocre officers to keep up the false prestige of *my boys doing well* ego syndrome. Do guard against that— you owe it to the organization and the good guys in other units. So work hard at raising the performance of your mediocre guys before they get into the region of reverse command (a term used in aerodynamics to highlight the inability of an engine to overcome excessive aerodynamic drag), or in simpler human terms, incompetence, and create problems for you. Therein lies your ability as a leader and motivator.

TAKING HARD DECISIONS

There are times when all your motivating skills fail, and much as you may dislike taking tough or harsh decisions, you are left with very little choice. The reason why this finds mention immediately after mediocrity and incompetence has to do with the Indian psyche. Taking tough decisions is alien to the Indian psyche, and so it is with us in the IAF. We always tend to associate 'hard or soft decisions with populism and the need for approval'. This, in turn, leads to 'flowing with the tide, path of least resistance and don't rock the boat' styles of commanding. The two main reasons for our inability to take tough decisions are:

- Fear of failure or 'why should I bell the cat' syndrome.
- Inability to manage conflict and criticism arising from the tough decision.

The key to taking tough decisions lies in your commitment to the organization and your unit, vis-à-vis your commitment to individuals or yourself. If you want to follow a path of least resistance and flow with the tide, go ahead; but remember! When you look back at your two years in command, you will wonder: Did I do anything worthwhile at all? If you are commanding a flying unit, your reluctance to take a tough decision could end up in your acting as a pall-bearer — I am sure no clarifications are needed here. A random list of some tough decisions is discussed subsequently, scrutiny of which will reveal that they are nothing extraordinary and would, in all probability, evoke a reaction from you of; "Hey! This is nothing new, it ought to have been implemented in the normal course of things". It is precisely these so-called normal decisions that do not get implemented very often unless focused upon specifically. Some of these related to operations are:

- **Weeding out of incompetent or unsafe aircrew:** No big deal, many would say, but ground realities are quite different at times. How often have we heard instructors in Flying Training Establishments say after reading about an accident in the squadrons: "Hey! I remember that I had recommended this chap for suspension/re-streaming, but he was pushed through", or a Squadron Cdr lamenting over red-tapism, which often results in delays in weeding out incompetent aircrew. To obviate the ill-effects of having disgruntled aircrew or officers and men remaining in a unit because of delays in decision making by command or Air HQ, the most preferred action is to keep the aircrew away from high-risk missions like air combat, and wait for him to get posted out, or get him posted if you have an extension counter in the personnel branch at Air Headquarters (commonly known as 'P' Staff).
- **Withdrawal of Rating/Supervisory Status:** This too is seldom done, though to be fair to the establishment, the Aircrew Examining Board and other monitoring organizations sometimes do come down heavily and do a job that should be done at unit level itself.
- **Decisions Related to Flying Environment:** At times, one finds that agencies responsible for providing you with a safe and congenial flying environment,

fail to do so. You can be accommodating up to a certain point and no more. The moment flight safety gets jeopardized, put your foot down, even at the cost of antagonizing your Chief Operations Officer and becoming unpopular on the station. Rest assured, your stand will be vindicated in the long run.

In a technology-intensive service as ours, correct maintenance practices hold the key to safety and longevity of equipment. From a CO's point of view, some areas that would demand your attention and necessitate a few tough decisions are:

- Adherence to correct maintenance practices and insisting on the checklist culture.
- Cleaning of aircraft, starting aggregates, radars, vehicles and ground equipment is another area where you have to be a *nag*, much to the chagrin of your Senior Technical Officer.
- The quantum of flying in the IAF is amongst the highest in the world and we have displayed a tendency to *flog ac, at times without good reason*. This trend needs to be checked, as flying hours too need to be preserved so that some congruity exists between calendar life and airframe life.
- We do have a tendency to overlook minor snags, especially in fleets with a poor overall serviceability, and have them rectified at the end of the day. Where do we draw the line? This is a dilemma facing every CO and to condemn it outright detaches you from ground realities. Do play your cards carefully.

EMPATHY—DO YOU HAVE IT?

How many times have you patiently listened to an alcoholic's problems? Would you go out of your way to push a request from an officer/airman/NC(E) for a posting on compassionate grounds? How would you tackle bereavement in the squadron family or the widow of one of your pilots, who is no more amongst you? In all such situations, the one quality needed in abundance as a leader is empathy — not mere lip service but real empathy in which you feel the others pain and anguish and genuinely listen and try to understand the person's need. Remember that empathy is not sympathy; the latter is a condescending way of clucking and saying ,"Hush, I know what's wrong — we understand your pain but it is something you have to take in your stride". The former, on the other hand, dovetails an understanding of the problem or the grief with willingness to help solve the problem, or alleviate the grief. Take, for instance, the case of a hard-working and sincere Sergeant, whose wife was suffering from a chronic hip and back problem that had left her bedridden for the past two years.

Relying on homoeopathy and Ayurveda after years of conventional treatment had not given her any relief, and the Sergeant was pressing for a compassionate grounds posting to Allahabad so that he could be close to his hometown and homoeopath. Not having any medical documents to strengthen his case, it would have been quite easy to reject his application. However, we advised the Sergeant to make a trip to the Research and Referral Hospital in Delhi and consult the orthopaedic and neuro surgeons instead of continuing with homoeopathy. Luckily, the specialists zeroed in on the problem and recommended a hip replacement, which was conducted successfully. The Sergeant was attached to Palam for three months and then posted to Safdarjung so that his wife could be rehabilitated at RR hospital. We, i.e. the Adjutant, STO and myself, did not do very much; we just approached the problem as our own and what we reaped was a lady who got back on her feet and a Sergeant who, hopefully, will serve the air force with dedication for years to come.

Many of our operational units are located in remote places where the environment is fairly hostile and living conditions are tough. There are many times when your officers and men work beyond the call of duty without asking for much. This is where empathy in the right dosage can act as a force multiplier. A smile, an enquiry about the family, spontaneous financial assistance to needy enrolled Non Combatants or NC(E)s as they are called from the Squadron Fund, and many such small gestures do wonders for the morale of a unit. As a CO, why? As human beings in general, we always expect something in return for any good deed or act done. If you want to display empathy, don't expect anything in return. Therein lies the uniqueness of empathy and why it is in such short supply.

ON SETTING AN EXAMPLE AND
LEADING FROM THE FRONT

In these changing times, one thing has not changed — the maxim of leading from the front. There is no other way to harness the full potential of your unit. At times COs are reluctant to lead from the front and adopt a proactive approach to command because of the following reasons:

- Lack of confidence, not lack of ability
- Fear of failure or even of making a mistake
- Not wanting to interfere for fear of curbing the initiative of subordinates.
  In the first two cases it is a lack of self-belief, while in the last one it could be

either a lack of commitment due to various reasons, or a lack of decision-making ability. If anyone can say that in his years of command, he has not experienced these pangs of doubt at some stage or the other, I will gift him an original Superman suit, lifted from Christopher Reeve's personal collection. What is important is to cast these vignettes of self-doubt away and set yourself simple and achievable things to do! Things that you had always wanted your CO to do in order to look up to him. Some simple actions that have an immediate effect on your position in your team are:

- Be amongst the first to fly in marginal weather.
- Don't shy away from range or air combat sorties in a fighter squadron or comparably difficult missions in the transport or helicopter fleets.
- Volunteer to share the workload of your Flight Commander if you find him over-worked or over-stressed.
- Help out with paper work whenever possible.
- Do parade, attend and play games with your men and officers and run the Physical Fitness Runs regularly with them.
- Do not put yourself on a pedestal. You can be *one of the guys* too and yet

command and not demand respect.

- Take tough decisions from time to time as it is important to dispel a 'soft guy image' if it appears at all.
- Honesty and integrity permeate downwards. Display them in every sphere, especially in financial matters and moral standards.
- Credibility is very important—don't promise your subordinates the moon, but deliver whatever you promise.

So, partner! Go ahead and seek your glory, but do it the right way and it will have a lasting effect.

LETTER TO THE DIRECTOR FLIGHT SAFETY

Air Chief Marshal I H Latif (Retd)PVSM

'Riyaaz'
House No. 6-3-248/4
Road No. 1 Banjara Hills,
Hyderabad - 500 034
Andhra Pradesh

27 Apr, 02

Dear Yajurvedi,

Just back from a wonderful holiday with my daughter and her little family in Shanghai to find the April issue of Flight Safety Magazine awaiting me. As always, I put everything aside to go thru' it from cover to cover! – and what a rewarding experience it was. How well, how very well you and your team have put it together, and what excellent articles – well written and so meaningful. Your idea of putting together all the articles of Subramaniam on leadership was also a very good one. I have taken them all out and intend to send them to my two sons in New York because what subramaniam has said has relevance to every occupation in which human beings play a role at work and at home!

My congratulations to all of you, and you have my warmest good wishes – you and your team.

Sincerely,

Air Cmde VK Yajurvedi VM
Director Flight Safety
Air HQ(RK Puram)
New Delhi 110 066

A FLIGHT SAFETY GUIDE FOR FLIGHT COMMANDERS

A Flight Commander of a squadron is the 2I/C and is responsible for implementing the KRAs of the Squadron Commander. These KRAs would reflect very succinctly, the KRAs of the IAF and have to be implemented both in letter and spirit. This is a daunting task and calls for a combination of professional expertise, management techniques and most important, a human touch. The Flight Commander is the 'man on the spot' — the very pulse of any operational outfit and this article is a tribute to him.

As I was rummaging through some old *Flight Safety* magazines, I came across this article, which I had written after completing my tenure as a flight commander. Flipping through it, I said to myself, "Hey! This is exactly what I monitored as CO", but on a different plane, as I left the execution of these paradigms of flight safety to my Flight Commander. At times, you may have an inexperienced or relatively junior Flight Commander who needs to be guided for a few months till he grasps the nuances and tricks of his trade. For this, you need to fall back on your own experiences in that chair. Every bit of what is discussed in the subsequent article is relevant, time tested and possible to implement. So do read on!

Having completed a reasonably long and relatively 'safe' tenure as the Flight Commander of a T-96 squadron, I am convinced of the need to adopt a 'holistic' and integrated approach towards flight safety. The only way you can achieve this is by involving yourself totally in whatever happens in the squadron. There is nothing about which you can turn around and say, "That is not my baby". There are some areas, like operations, where you can directly intervene and influence; some areas, like maintenance and welfare of men, where you need to establish a good rapport with your technical officers and senior Non Commissioned Officers; and some areas, like gauging and keeping track of the emotional and physical well being of your pilots, which depend on the relationship you establish with them. I firmly believe that experiences in the field need to be shared before they fade into pleasant memories; I thought I'd bring out a number of thumb rules, cardinal sins and useful tips that could greatly enhance flight safety.

Operations

Safe conduct of flying operations without diluting operational efficiency should be on the top of any list of KRAs for a Flight Commander. The first step is to compartmentalize each aspect of flying operations. Decide on aspects that you will ensure and not compromise on and then amalgamate them into an overall plan for daily flying. This will ensure that you do not miss out on important aspects, particularly during busy days. The various compartments I made for myself were:

- Under-training flying
- Air-to-ground training
- Air combat training
- Flying on detachments and exercises
- Flying discipline
- Tackling the weather

Under Training

Get to know your new pilots; for which you need to talk to them like a friend so that they open out to you in the first instance and come out with their hopes, fears and, if you are lucky, their weaknesses and problems. Some critical issues that you need to closely monitor are:

- Carry out a thorough perusal of old blue books and log books.
- Ring up their previous Flight Commanders and enquire about their general performance.
- Monitor performance in pre-flight training.
- Fly at least one pre-solo Dual Check with them.
- If in doubt about their capability to go solo, do not hesitate to fly another Dual Check with them or ask the CO to fly them.
- Closely monitor approach and landing techniques for at least 20 sorties. Don't worry about being a nag initially; nip the wrong tendencies in the bud.
- Watch their attitude towards checks and procedures; it reveals a lot.
- Gradually evolve a counselling technique for each pilot; some need to be cajoled, some need incessant nagging and some learn when told once.

Air-to-Ground Training

Range work (Air–to-Ground Firing) is the bread and butter of all ground attack squadrons. It is an area that demands close supervision. The potential danger areas one has to look out for are:

- Target fixation and controlled flight into the ground
- Low pullouts

- Debris damage
- Over stressing the aircraft
- Fuel discipline
- Navigation to range
- Crew room banter and claims.

How then can you ensure safe conduct of range work and at the same time achieve consistent scores? Easier said than done! So what? It has to be done.

- Conduct regular phase briefs and refresher briefs even at the cost of being repetitive.
- Standardise and do not accept any deviations, especially from relatively inexperienced pilots.
- Scrutinize flight data recorders regularly and pull up offenders.
- Analyse weapon camera films regularly and ask your Fighter Strike Leader to look into nascent errors, like firing ranges and dive angles.
- Set an example over range. You need to dispel the age-old misnomer that good results can only be achieved by going in close.
- Even if you personally, as the flight commander, are going through a lean

phase, do not absolve yourself of the need to keep a check! I have myself experienced a reluctance to tick off a gung-ho youngster in such a situation; as a result, the next day he was sent back from range after a low pull-out.

- Ration your praise for good scores and do not openly berate poor scores. If you don't, overconfidence and over trying may be the net result; consequences of which are well known.
- Discuss emergencies over range regularly, particularly engine-related ones.

Air Combat Training

Lack of aids, like Air Combat Manoeuvring Instrumentation and Airborne Video Tracking Recorders makes the monitoring of air combat an extremely difficult proposition. The speed and manoeuvrability of modern high performance aircraft demands a pilot to be physically fit and alert. He needs to be in the correct frame of mind and eager to fight. Therefore, instinct, judgment and aggression are the keys to air combat. These facts are the cause of accidents too and if this is understood, half your battle against accidents during or after combat would be won. Here is how you could go about it!

- Progress your youngster slowly during the basic air combat phase, specially if it is his first operational squadron, irrespective of whether he is a fast learner or a slow starter. You will come under pressure from various quarters. Succumb to them and there goes flight safety! The choice is entirely yours.
- Monitor every pilot closely during combat, including yourself. Your KRA should be able to guage the combat worthiness of every pilot in the squadron in terms of his strengths and weakness within 4–6 months. This will give you at least a year to work on the team as a whole.
- Ensure that you fly at least one sortie with the experienced pilots and two with the rookies every month.
- Specially watch out for aspects like overstressing the aircraft, poor spotting, over-confidence, over-excited Radio Transmission (RT), tongue-tied RT, poor regroups and poor landings after a combat sortie. All these are potential ingredients of an accident.
- Co-opt the squadron Fighter Combat Leader/Fighter Strike Leader/Pilot Attack Instructor in this mission of yours. Remember that he is the specialist and give him his due. Having a motivated and dedicated professional around you, irrespective of seniority, is a great help.
- Be selectively critical during debriefs without compromising on safety aspects; be careful when you censure a combat pilot in public and be stingy with praise.

- Do not hesitate to review/ stop a pilot's progress if he is dangerous during air combat, or if he repeatedly flouts flight safety restrictions.

Detachments and Exercises

Detachments and exercises provide a flight commander with an excellent opportunity to get to know the lads and be one of them. However, an unfamiliar flying environment has resulted in many avoidable mishaps. Go prepared, be vigilant and stay focused during a detachment and you will come back home with your batteries recharged. Here is a 'safety checklist':

- Kill most of the briefings before the ferry out, specially the ones on airfield layout and the new and unfamiliar Local Flying Area.
- Lay down ground rules for conduct during the detachment. Do stress on projecting a good image.
- If possible, do not take guys with family problems; you could end up with a problem.
- Build up your flying effort gradually so as to peak mid-way through the detachment/exercise.
- Every detachment has a specific aim; stick to it as closely as possible. Avoid the temptation to catch up on routine tasks.
- Space out your flying schedule.
- Do not encourage extended working hours, specially during armament detachments or Dissimilar Air Combat Training camps. Even during exercises, pace yourselves during the work-up phase so that your aircrews are not fatigued by the time the main exercise starts.
- Encourage interaction with pilots of other squadrons/types. After every exercise/combined detachment, ask for suggestions and observations, which could improve the flying environment in your squadron.
- Detail a committed and sharp youngster to observe the attitude, approach and discipline of the other squadrons. It is always good to learn from others.
- As a flight commander, don't stay cocooned with the CO. Spend quality time with your youngsters, both at work and during leisure time, without being a pain. Apart from getting to know them better, you would be in a position to ensure that they do not go overboard, going on a binge on weekdays and having late nights.
- Encourage sports as a means of spending free time in the evenings. Many pilots do not get time at their parent bases to indulge in these, due to various reasons.

Flying Discipline

Flying-related discipline is paramount and all aspects discussed earlier would come to nought if the basics of discipline are not ingrained in your outfit. Why do I call it 'related'? Because what you need to look for is an attitude, a way of life and an inner discipline, all of which are essential for flying discipline or, for that matter, maintenance discipline. Here are a few tips for you to consider:

- Encourage transparency and honesty when it comes to admitting mistakes in the air and on the ground, which led to, or could have led to an accident/incident. I would like to narrate an incident, which drives the point home. A diligent, committed and professionally sound youngster touched his ventral fin on landing during the initial stages of his flying syllabus in his first operational squadron. Without fear, he immediately came to me and admitted that he had inadvertently throttled back to idle before touch-down and raised the attitude excessively in the process. By simply stating the obvious, the youngster did not realise the chain he was triggering. Since the facts were so readily available, there was no time wasted in finishing the Court of Inquiry. Command HQ was not agitated but merely expressed concern and asked the squadron to be more vigilant. The youngster flew a couple of Dual sorties to iron out minor flaws in his landing techniques and emerged from the incident unscathed. He also sent out a message to the rest that honesty pays and thankfully; quite a few came out with mistakes readily, allowing us to take remedial measures in time.
- Repetitive mistakes have to be punished. Don't get soft and repent later.
- Grounding a pilot for a few days is a harmless yet effective way of showing that you mean business.
- Be consistent in your approach of flying discipline. A good guy too has to get the same amount of stick. Reward him elsewhere.
- Tackle aircrew with an attitudinal problem firmly. Counsel them, give them time to respond positively, and if they fail to do so, don't hesitate to weed them out.
- Needless to say, set high personal standards of discipline in the air and on ground.

That's what leadership is all about.

Tackling Weather

Inability to recognise, respect and tackle weather has resulted in numerous accidents. Work out your own methods of weather indoctrination. A few tips in this area are as follows:

- Discuss weather frequently and build up a personal rapport with the Met Officer. Take his advice seriously and never mind the few occasions when his forecast is out.
- Do not neglect 'under the hood' flying, and insist on accuracy from pilots and controllers during instrument approaches.
- Gradually build up your pilot's ability to fly in visibility conditions down to their minima. Prior to this, satisfy yourself by flying them in the trainer.
- Advise your Senior Flying Supervisor, who oversees flying in the Air Traffic Control, to recall all aircraft in time, irrespective of the seniority of the pilots.
- Divert in time to an alternative base if the weather at your own base has deteriorated more rapidly than you had anticipated. For heaven's sake, instill in your pilots the confidence and courage to divert and make first-time approaches and landings.
- Discuss aquaplaning and disorientation repeatedly and share experiences of bad-weather flying.

Maintenance

With our diverse fleet mix, especially in fighter fleet, safe and effective maintenance assumes tremendous importance. As the flight commander, it is your direct responsibility to ensure that synergy exists between operations and maintenance. Only then can you ensure safe and effective utilisation of our ageing fighter fleet. Here are a few tips:

- Go out of your way to make the Engineering Officers feel that they matter and that their contribution is extremely vital.
- Don't hesitate to give them responsibility and hold them accountable too.
- First and second-line maintenance management and monitoring are the keys to maintenance safety.
- Have a total hold over snag analysis, monitoring and rectifications. Ask for a daily briefing on the same. Don't compromise on this, whatever be the pressures of work.
- Insist that the youngsters go out frequently to the tarmac and monitor servicing and rectifications. Apart from increasing their interaction with the men, it sends out a signal that somebody is watching.
- Do not accept aircraft with minor snags as far as possible. I am aware of the constraints but don't take chances.
- Stagger aircraft so that you don't flog a particular aircraft and fatigue it.
- Warrant Officers and Sergeants hold the key to effective and safe

maintenance practices. Give them responsibility and authority too. Very often have I seen them lose interest because their authority has been challenged by a junior airman, with little or no intervention by the supervising officer.

Human and Hygiene Factors

Today's high-performance aircraft demand a high state of mental and physical well-being. Neglect of these aspects can prove disastrous, as has been seen in a number of accidents. As the flight commander, one quality that you need in abundance is empathy. Only then can you be a friend and guide, to whom your youngsters will turn in times of emotional distress. Some areas that would demand your attention are:

- Accommodation
- Leave planning
- Personal problems, like pregnancy, small children, chronic illness of family members, marital discord, financial problems and alcoholism
- Even your airmen would benefit from your involvement in their daily lives. All they need is patient listening, interaction with a smile, participation in sports activity and occasional visits to the mess and billets.

Parting Shot

This was not meant to be a sermon, nor was I able to implement all that I have suggested. However, this certainly is a reaffirmation that you as the flight commander are the principal agent of flight safety and, come what may, you cannot absolve yourself of that responsibility. Over the years, reluctance to delegate responsibility has undermined the position of the flight commander. This trend has to reverse if we are to nurture responsible, mature and effective flight commanders who could act as flag-bearers of flight safety at the squadron level. The going will always be tough and you would have to don many hats during the course of a single day. Always remember that you represent the cutting edge of the air force. Lower your guard and the sword gets blunt!

WHAT ARE WE AFRAID OF?

The analysis of the human factors (HFACS) plays a very important role in accident investigation the world over. Issues like fatigue, though controversial, cannot be ignored if we are to create and maintain a safe flying environment. It is laudable that the IAF is coming to grips with the need to look closely at HFACS as a tool for improving accident investigation procedures. The two incidents highlighted below show that pilots are human and not supermen and have to be handled like glass, with care.

Wing Commander Taneja's 'Mail Bag' contribution on fatigue in aviation accidents in the April issue was extremely thought provoking and I asked myself, "Why did it have to be a doctor to address the issue first? Are we as a community of aviators too egoistic or afraid to open a Pandora's Box by talking about fatigue?" One of the probable reasons why aircrew fatigue is never indicated as a cause of accidents is because it may be unpalatable to the 'establishment' and Courts of Inquiry do not want to 'rock the boat'. In my moderately long career, I too have seen a number of accidents whose primary cause was undoubtedly fatigue, but due to reasons of expediency, may have been attributed to lack of situational awareness (SA) or disorientation.

Two accidents that occurred in the late 1980s and early 1990s immediately come to my mind, wherein indifference to fatigue and emotional well-being of the individual was the root cause of the accident. Although the final cause of both accidents was disorientation, the underlying emotional fatigue in one case and physical fatigue in the other could have led to the final disorientation. Both pilots were buddies from my first squadron, 'The Hawkeyes' — one a senior Squadron Leader and a Qualified Flying Instructor (QFI), whilst the other was a contemporary.

In the first case, the Squadron Leader was the Senior Flight Commander of an MiG-21 squadron. He was a volatile and high-strung individual in the midst of a divorce and custody battle that had been going on for quite a few years. Highly egoistic, like most fighter jocks, the officer resented any institutional intervention or interference as he called it in his personal matters and continued to fly actively and mind you, fly fairly well. There is no doubt in my mind that 'emotional fatigue' resulted in his sad end in a night-flying accident. What was the cause of the accident? — Probably disorientation. As a youngster I always wondered as to why the establishment never stepped in, stopped his flying and posted him on a ground tenure till he had sorted out his personal problems. Had it done so, we may have averted a 'disorientation' accident. What happened instead was that the pilot faced a situation that demanded his superior skills and 'came a cropper' because of emotional fatigue.

In the other case, a young fully ops Squadron Leader in a Jaguar Squadron got thoroughly disoriented during a night strike mission in marginal weather, got into a Cumulo Nimbus cloud patch (CB) and never came back. The Cockpit Voice Recorder (CVR) told a chilling story of a man literally fighting for his life. Once again it was a case of a pilot's inability to harness his superior skills, which should have accrued after years of multi aircraft training because of sheer physical fatigue.

The scenario was different in this case. A command-level exercise was being conducted in a command that generally was not known for conducting regular exercises and squadrons were 'pushed' to the limit — fair enough, because that is what one expects during actual operations. However, adequate rest prior to a late-night ground attack mission is considered absolutely essential, be it in peace or war. In this particular case, the officer had flown extensively (two or three sorties by day) and did express his reservation about flying in marginal weather conditions by night, but then probably gave in to his ego and went for the mission, never to come back. Here was a clear case of physical fatigue leading to disorientation, caused by entry into inclement weather. Here too, the officer was a stubborn type, who prided himself on his physical toughness — how could he, of all people tell his comrades that he was tired or sceptical of flying in those conditions? Once again, the question that arises is, why did not people up the chain intervene and question the rationale of launching the mission in marginal weather, that too by night? Food for thought, I guess.

During his recent farewell visit to our base, an Air Officer Commanding-in-Chief narrated his impressions on accident analysis and prevention in the United States Air Force (USAF), which reflected the transparency and honesty that is required in any drive to reduce accidents and promote learning. As Commandant of the IAF's prestigious Tactics and Combat Development Establishment, the Air Marshal, then a Group Captain had visited a parallel establishment in the USAF, where he was presented with a video cassette that depicted three live pull-outs from a range sortie. The first pull-out was a perfectly executed manoeuvre, the second one a delayed pull-out that would send shivers down any aviator's spine and the third one was a live recording of a 'no pull-out' and classic target fixation case with all the associated pull-out radio calls that were ignored and resulted in the pilot just flying into the ground. When queried whether they would really like him to keep the cassette, the Yanks remarked that if it would help save lives, they really did not care about image projection. The point I am trying to drive home here is that 'the whole truth and nothing but the truth' is what we need to digest, and not just 'part of the truth'; and aircrew fatigue is certainly one element of the truth that is generally missed out. In this part, I will discuss certain live issues, like fatigue identification, cases of emotional and physical fatigue, and the core issue of when to say 'No' and 'Stop'. Fatigue identification goes far beyond the 'red eye syndrome' and presents a great challenge to both doctors and squadron supervisors. With social norms changing rapidly and officers guarding their personal space fiercely, it has become extremely difficult for Flight Commanders and COs to continuously track the composite emotional and physical well-being of aircrew. With the strength of aircrew in Air Superiority Fighter squadrons on the rise, the problem would only be compounded over the next few years. In an earlier article of mine, which comes next — 'Where are you, Buddy?' — I have lamented on the absence of a buddy culture in our squadrons today. Let me tell you, these buddies also played a vital role in ensuring that nagging ailments and worries, signs of fatigue that a youngster would try to hide and any emotional disturbances, were relayed discreetly up the chain to the Flight Commander, who, would unobtrusively send us off on leave or take us off the flying programme on the pretext of a pressing secondary duty.

What are the signs that one needs to look for to identify the onset of fatigue? I have divided these signs into primary or physical signs of fatigue and tertiary/perceptive signs of fatigue. The former are easy to identify whilst the latter demand certain qualities, like care, concern, empathy and the overriding aspect of flight safety, which says that if a pilot is not mentally or physically fit, he just does not fly.

Primary Signs

- **Signs of sleep deprivation** due to various reasons, ranging from anxiety to troublesome babies or late-night partying. The most common signs would be red eyes, dark circles under the eyes or excessive yawning during briefings.
- **Excessive weight loss** is a modern-day manifestation of stress and needs to be monitored carefully. Dietary control in the case of slightly overweight pilots, has also been known to cause fatigue and uncontrolled and indiscriminate exercise schedules need to be monitored from time to time.
- **Increased susceptibility to minor ailments, like cough and cold.**
- **Sudden dip in professional performance** could be a result of fatigue caused due to overwork or 'pushing a high performer too hard', or a low performer beyond the limits of his capabilities.
- **Sudden tendency to take shortcuts.**

Tertiary signs

Sometimes it is extremely difficult to fathom what is going on in the human mind and pilots are very human, very vulnerable to stresses and fatigue, the likes of which very few professions experience. As supervisors and leaders, we need to continuously update ourselves on the latest trends in aviation psychology and not leave it just to the Aviation Medicine specialists to periodically caution us on various issues. Some of the less visible signs of fatigue that could prove useful to supervisors at the squadron level are listed below; do pay heed to them!

- Frequent loss of temper
- Withdrawn behaviour from an otherwise cheerful person
- Poor crew resource management or CRM in multi crew platforms
- Despondent talk.

Saying No

One of the weakest areas in our service is our inability to say no, both as individuals and as an organization in areas relating to flight safety. That we train for war during peacetime is an inescapable reality of military aviation. However, what has to be seen side by side is that we need to preserve resources too so that they are available for war, and one of the means of preservation is to identify and nip fatigue in the bud. Acknowledging that he is tired, fatigued or under-prepared for a mission because of fatigue is one of the hardest things for an aviator to do, but in the interests of flight safety, time and again we need to impress on this motley and egoistic 'creature' that he too is human and fallible. I am not saying for one moment that we need to breed sissies — all we need to do is to have the guts to say no at all levels. A young pilot should have the guts to tell his flight commander that he is fatigued; a CO should have the guts to tell his AOC that a particular mission during an exercise will not be possible because his aircrew have flown their quota for the day and a Chief Operations Officer should be able to advise Command staff of ground realities whenever things seem to be going out of hand. From what I understand of the new generation, they are far more mature when it comes to operating within their limitations and capabilities — they will speak up if they are physically fatigued or tired. What we need to watch out for is the psychological and emotional fatigue that is well concealed in today's complex inter-personal relationships that exist in squadrons.

If you are tired, mate — Speak up
or else you may be fighting to
save your skin in a situation that
demands your superior skill.
On the flip side mate,
don't make it a habit to say you are tired
coz that makes you a sissy and we don't
need no sissies in cockpits. So mate,
be wise n make your choice—you know best.

MANAGEMENT BY WANDERING AROUND
A POWERFUL TOOL OF FLIGHT SAFETY

This article deals with the topic of the Chief Operations Officer, or the COO, as he is popularly known and his areas of responsibility. It covers very simply the power of observation and mobility. The article strongly argues the case for a 'hands-on style of management' as a tool for creating and maintaining a safe flying environment at any flying base.

All of you know about that prized creature, the MBA. Most of you would have had to tolerate MBO or Management by Objectives during management capsules somewhere along your careers. The more progressive amongst you guys must be practising Management of Change within your own spheres of influence. But MBWA (Management By Wandering Around) — 'What nonsense!' — I can hear some of you saying. Believe me when I say that MBWA can be an incisive and effective tool in improving flight safety on a station. I happened to lay my eyes on this concept whilst reading an article on Managing Change by Prof. CK Prahalad, a revered management guru at the University of Michigan. My interpretation of all corporate success stories that have been built on this concept boils down to the following principles:

- Mobility of the top management
- Observation
- Feedback
- Conversion capability of the top management of their observation and feedback they receive into processes and products.

Without wandering too much, let me share my conviction with you, that only if the top management on a station wanders around will there be change. Let me stick to the Chief Operations Officer's wandering around and leave the others to take their own walk in their own styles. The ideal time to start wandering around is early morning, a few minutes before morning Met briefing. What is it that you would observe?

- **Is the FOD parade being conducted meticulously? For those of you who are a little foxed by this term, FOD stands for Foreign Object Damage and deals with damage caused to an aircraft engine when it picks up stray objects, like stones, nuts, etc. which may be lying around on the operating surfaces due to** neglect. Ensuring that these surfaces are absolutely clean is the COO's job. Before flying commences, the runways and taxi tracks are scanned physically by men to ensure that stray objects are picked up.

- **Are the men merely ambling along the RW or looking down to pick up FOD?**
- **What is the extent of small bird activity?**
- **One look at the sky would also give you a likely weather picture for the forenoon.**

The next important time-slot to wander around in is between 1–2 hours after Met briefing. This time round a different set of issues could be observed.

- **Are the manoeuvring areas absolutely ready for the day's flying?**
- **Are controllers alert and ready on R/T ? Is the crash crew correctly on station?**
- **Are aircraft on the ground following correct procedures, like maintaining correct taxiing distance and departure procedures?**
- **Are the bird shooters responsive and in position?**

Military Engineering Service support to operations on a daily basis is essential and encompasses varied functions, ranging from routine joint filling of cracks on the runway surface, epoxy work or filling small joints, clearance of runways and taxi-tracks, to the manning of generator sets that are so very important to provide standby power supply.

- **Are the tractors and labourers on station or have they done the vanishing act well before lunch time?**
- **Is the joint filling and epoxy work being carried out as per specifications? Is there a supervisor around? Is the compound at the right temperature etc?**
- **It would also give you an opportunity to monitor the bird activity and check the response of the Bird Hazard Combat Teams.**
- **Monitor a few talk-down approaches on the walkie talkie, and some landings. This would give you a fair idea of the synergy that exists between aircrew and your controllers.**
- **Run up to the ATC or go across to the radar to chat up your controllers and Met officers, especially when the traffic is heavy or the weather is marginal and flying/recoveries are in progress.**

Having made your presence felt around the operating environment around mid-day, the next 'probe' around last landing time would comprise the

following checks:

- **Bird activity**
- **Adherence to last landing time and ground-run timings**
- **Preparations for night flying**
- **Adherence to timings for flare-path layout**
- **Night flying briefing and interaction with ATC personnel.**

Not for one moment am I suggesting that as the COO you need to be on the move all the time. Spread your time slots across the week and you will find that you would have a pretty good grasp of all that is going on under your nose. Additionally, it will give you enough ammunition to keep people on their toes.

Advantages of MBWA

MBWA is nothing but an acronym for a hands-on style of management that is so necessary for effective control and supervision of the operating environment at any base. Detractors of this style may say that it involves too much interference and lack of delegation. This is not true at all as you are just wandering around, observing and absorbing the environment with the aim of advising and providing critical inputs aimed at plugging potential problem areas. Far too many times have we seen an accident or incident taking place because of an environmental lapse — it could be a bird hit because an otherwise vigilant SFS&IO had lowered his guard for a few days or an FOD incident that could have occurred because a normally meticulous SATCO had missed out an area that needed epoxy work or joint filling or a collision on the runway because a traffic crossing point was left open by a DATCO due to pre-occupation with controlling. In all the above cases, a wandering COO may have been able to back up his team with vital inputs by virtue of his wanderlust.

Conversion Capability

All this wandering around will come to nought if you cannot impress on your team the need to convert inputs and feedback into processes, products or action. A classic example is how speedily you react to a situation wherein you suddenly notice an increase in bird activity at a particular time or in a particular area with a number of ac in the air. Does your flight safety officer and his team have the ability to:

- Analyse the cause of sudden increase in bird activity?
- Deploy additional bird shooters at short notice?
- Muster up a Quick Reaction Team to send bird shooters outside the airfield if required?
- Identify unauthorized carcass disposal and lodge FIRs with the police?
- Have the mechanism and the ability to interact with the village sarpanch and panchayat?

If all these efforts pay off and don't hamper your flying, it is the result of 'wandering around'. Many such contingencies would receive proactive intervention if vital decisions are taken at critical times and these decisions would be forthcoming from your team if they know exactly what you expect from them.

So, pal! Don't be a paper tiger as Chief Operations Officer — rule-bound and chair-borne most of the time — weighed down by the diktats of your 'boss' and command. Don't be a nostalgic 'stick throttle' type either, who merely zips down to the squadron, flies a couple of sorties and reminisces about 'My days' — be instead, a wanderer in your Gypsy! Only then can you contribute effectively in making your operating environment safer and more effective. As usual, I would like to sign off by saying that nothing that I have articulated is new; it is just packaged differently, with the hope that it motivates all you 'harassed' COOs to keep going at it. Remember, you can make one helluva difference by just wandering around.

MURPHY STRIKES AGAIN
ENCOUNTERS OF THE SUKHOI-30 KIND

The Chief Operations Officer's job is fraught with a fair element of risk, and as is true of all matters concerning aviation, Murphy's Law, which governs the possibility of something going wrong despite all risks being covered, hangs ominously over his head. This anecdote covers it all! The anecdote was published in The IAF's Flight Safety journal as part of their Human Error Voluntary Reporting Series.

Bareilly was abuzz with excitement in March 2004. The big birds had finally arrived and the station was all geared up to cope with the increased flying that was bound to follow. As a background to what was going to unfold, the previous year had seen a lull of flying activity at Bareilly due to various reasons, prime amongst them being intense bird activity and inclement weather. Time and again, the Air Officer Commanding (AOC) had cautioned me about the likely fallout of this inactivity and impressed on me the need for close supervision through briefings and strict control of the flying environment.

All the Air Traffic Controllers (ATCOs) were a wee bit rusty (not their fault at all) and in the absence of a Senior ATCO, supervision was a trifle difficult. A thorough briefing for all ATC and radar controllers was organized by the Squadron, emphasizing the peculiarities of arrival/departure procedures of the SU-30, and operations in general. One of the peculiarities of SU-30 departures was that only the No.1 in a formation asked for line-up and take-off while the rest of the formation streamed in without any R/T calls. No formation take-offs were permitted and ac lined up singly for departure at an interval of 30 seconds to one minute as an anti-FOD precaution. There was no flying on the day of briefing and only one controller was left behind for Tower duties whilst the rest of his colleagues scribbled away on their notepads. I distinctly remember having told the SATCO to ensure that the lone controller missing from briefing was briefed thoroughly about the difference in take-off procedures for SU-30.

That's when Lord Murphy decided to get into the act. The next day dawned bright and clear — it had to be — since it was going to be the first day of SU-30 operations at Bareilly. There was the normal hustle and bustle around the ATC, with bird watchers and runway controllers being deployed and vehicular movement around the manoeuvering areas, pretty heavy. The radar controller had to be dropped at the GCA cabin; off he went on the ATC vehicle with his ·

two-way radio set — "Permission to cross runway" — "Clear cross runway". At the same time four SU-30s taxied out and I too left my office to witness the first SU-30 departures from Bareilly. All seemed fine when Titus–1 asked for line-up and then take-off. As No.1 took off, the LMV with only the MTD asked for permission on his two-way radio set to cross the R/W and return to the Crash Bay. Looking to his right, the DATCO saw the second SU-30 moving forward to line up and must have said to himself, "He will now line up and ask for take-off; in the meantime let me allow our ATC vehicle to cross". DATCO on R/T — "ATC vehicle clear cross". The ATC vehicle was still about 10–20 m from the runway edge when the SU-30 started rolling for take-off, not noticed by the ATC vehicle. By the time the aircraft had crossed about 500 metres, the pilot noticed the vehicle on the runway and calmly gave a call "vehicle on the runway" — continuing with the take-off and lifted off perilously close to and over the ATC vehicle. I was standing in front of the ATC and froze! Thank God it was an SU-30, which unstuck in clean configuration well short of the MM (the intersection is close to Middle Marker)! Had it been an MiG-21or 25, it would have been curtains for all of us.

What went wrong

- The Duty ATCO (DATCO) on duty was the DATCO who had not attended the SU-30 brief. Murphy ensured that his colleagues did not brief him.
- Habit interference caused a mismatch between sensory perception and ground reality — the young DATCO kept muttering in shock, "But he never asked for take-off".
- Runway crossing by ATC vehicles equipped with two-way radio sets becomes a necessity at times. This time it was unnecessary. The vehicle should have been instructed to wait for all departures.
- All of us got away by the skin of our teeth, thanks to the pilot, who retained his cool, knew his aircraft well and unstuck a trifle early but with adequate margin. Luck got the better of Murphy in the end — others may not be so lucky another time, therefore
- Watch those changes in procedures when new ac operate at your base.
- Insist on refresher briefings on peculiarities of a new ac to be covered during met briefings.
- Closely monitor vehicular traffic around ac manoeuvring areas. Stick to FOD lanes (these lanes are marked at all airfields to clearly demarcate lanes for vehicular traffic) and as far as possible cross the runway at crossing points only.

- Why can't we have underground runway crossing points, like they have at many airfields abroad? Till then, we need to press hard for a network of good perimeter roads so that all vehicular traffic can be routed only on perimeter roads.
- Situational awareness remains as essential as ever — ensure that your ground support staff inculcates it. Prudence demanded that the MTD waited till all ac took off, instead, he was in a tearing hurry to get back to the crash bay instead of just relaxing on the other side of the runway and enjoying the sight of the magnificent birds taking off.

WHERE ARE YOU, BUDDY?
MENTORING AND FLIGHT SAFETY

Notwithstanding the accidents caused due to technical defects in the recent past, Human Error remains a vexing issue. One aspect of Human Error that poses the greatest problem for COs and Flight Commanders is SUPERVISION. Today, supervision has become so structured and rule-bound, that squadrons seem to have forgotten the art of informal or relaxed supervision. In our relentless search for implementable ideas and techniques to enhance flight safety, mentoring has seldom featured in our various flight safety programmes. Maybe it is time now to take a closer look at this concept that is being debated in a number of armed forces as a tool for enhancing leadership qualities, reducing human error and putting years of experience to immediate use rather than digging them out of the archives when it is too late.

Mentoring is not new to the IAF; it has existed in various forms, the most common one that I can recollect being the 'Buddy concept' in various squadrons at junior levels. Moving up the chain of command and seniority, mentoring has been looked upon with suspicion and associated with negative

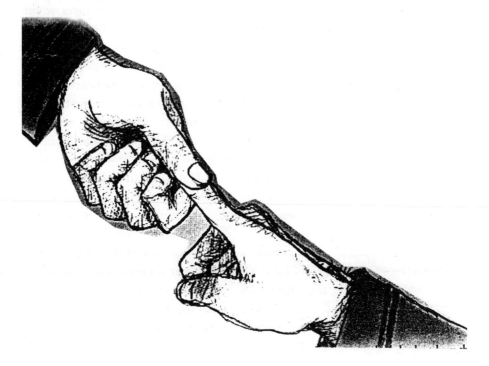

traits like sycophancy, or being a blue-eyed boy or part of a privileged club or lobby if one stayed in touch with senior officers with whom one has served. More of that later, for it is time to establish a link between flight safety and mentoring. As a youngster in my first squadron, The Hawkeyes, I recollect having been exposed to a very healthy system of mentoring. The squadron was recovering from two fatal accidents attributable to Disorientation and Human Error during air combat. A premature change in command had taken place and the morale was visibly affected. Six of us, raw, but eager fighter jocks, trooped in from Tezpur and Kalaikunda after finishing our MiG and Hunter conversions, eager to learn our trade in our first operational squadron. The strength of the squadron at that time was a strong duo at the top and a committed bunch of young Flight Lieutenants and Flying Officers. Together they raised the performance of the squadron to more than acceptable levels with no further accidents. When I look back at how the squadron managed to groom six pilot officers, 'good mentoring' was the key. Each one of us had a buddy who was totally responsible not only for his own performance but also that of his buddy. Andy, Pulak, Rags, Chatto, Ramsy and Baveja knew everything there was to know about the six of us, with Mo, Radha, Tats and Karan providing the second tier of mentoring when the first tier needed bolstering. The system worked well and was based on trust, accountability, concern and squadron interest. I can recollect a number of instances when genuine aviation errors were rectified at the 'buddy level'. Low pullouts, dragging approaches, fast taxiing and a host of other common Under Training errors having accident potential were ruthlessly monitored, pointed out, discussed and ironed out at a much lower level. Mentoring did not end at work; it continued in the MiG Alley (Bachelors, Block), permeated into the bar and continued at home. On the face of it, our buddies were just about two years senior to us and they were only Flying Officers. But what made them so effective was the enormous responsibility given to them and the knowledge of what lack of supervision could lead to! The buddy concept has been loosely practised in other squadrons as well, but has never been institutionalized. The benefits of the buddy system were numerous. Amongst the major ones were:

- Creation of a 'multiple tier' of monitoring and counselling that comprised the buddy, the squadron QFI/FCL, the Flight Commander and finally, the CO.
- Responsibility made the Flying Officer/Flight Lieutenant reach aviation maturity much earlier. Not that he did not take mistakes; he did, but they were more related to over-confidence against non-adherence to basic procedures and airmanship.

- The buddy system fosters healthy camaraderie and creates the foundation for a lasting relationship within the service. It exposes young officers to the benefits of commitment and concern at a very early age of their careers.
- At the end of the day, mentoring and the buddy system made the Hawkeyes a safety conscious squadron.

Mentoring is possible only when the mentor is well qualified (at least fully Ops), well motivated (hard to quantify) and focused on the profession of aviation. What one sees today is that mentoring at a junior level has reduced significantly and that the Medium Level supervisor is no longer as effective as he used to be. How has this affected flight safety? Flight Commanders and COs are bogged down by basic supervision, with very little time for other pressing issues related to tactics and operational development. Why has the first tier of mentoring/guidance/supervision collapsed? Some reasons could be:

- Too early a change in the type of the first fighter aircraft, leading to lack of consolidation, and confidence on any one type; do remember that confidence/self assurance is one of the key ingredients to good mentoring and supervision.
- Preoccupation with marriage and asset building, caused by environmental pressures and compulsions, has reduced the amount of time that a Fully Ops 2 ac leader spends with the younger lot. This was not the case 15–20 years ago when professional status, healthy competition amongst peers and consolidation were very important for a Medium Level supervisor. Whom do we blame? Certainly not the individual alone! It is possible that the organization has focused wrongly on what is expected from an aircrew of 4–7 years of service; perhaps, too much emphasis has been placed on individual professional development and chasing courses and too little on motivational aspects and subordinate development. When one looks at the profile of this category of aircrew, this is what one observes:
- On achieving a Fully Ops status — the race is on to achieve 2 ac lead and migrate on to Air Superiority Fighters (ASFs). On the personal front, it is time for bride hunting and raising a family. Result — stress, distraction, preoccupation, no time to spend with the next rung of Under-Training pilots.
- On transition to ASFs — the young Flight Lieutenant finds himself at the bottom end of the learning curve again and by the time he is Fully Ops, it is time to go to the Flying Instructors' School. As a Qualified Flying Instructor now, he becomes a mentor or teacher with very little earlier experience in informal mentoring. Has it affected the QFI's performance?

- It is only when this QFI returns to a squadron with 10–11 years of service at the earliest, that he takes on the role of serious mentoring and developing youngsters. What has been the result of the erosion of the first tier of supervision or mentoring?

Some are highlighted below:

- Excessive involvement of Flight Commander and CO in basic supervision.
- Communication gap between the Under-Training pilots and senior supervisors resulting from a generation divide.
- Increased accidents caused by supervisory lapses resulting from an overload on the system.
- Small mistakes being overlooked or hidden at times, leading to avoidable mishaps. These mistakes would normally have been observed by the buddy and pointed out in time, had such a system continued. If one looks at a similar seniority bracket in the army, one looks at a Company Commander with excellent exposure to subordinate development and bubbling with confidence. We need such a bunch to share the workload of senior supervisors in a squadron. The revitalisation of this segment of aircrew is bound to have a positive impact on flight safety. What can we do to give more teeth to our first tier of supervision?
- Let us formally revive the 'buddy' system, assign clear-cut responsibilities and seriously assess these Fully Ops/2ac leaders/ML supervisors for leadership and subordinate development.
- Try and ensure a minimum stay of four years in the first Op squadron and three years in a subsequent ASF squadron/two years in a similar type squadron. FIS eligibility could be 7 years for aircrew who have stayed on a single type and 8 years for those who have two types under their belt. This would also improve the quality of QFIs. A loose structure that is by no means without loopholes, is outlined below.

1st SQUADRON :
2 years to Fully Ops + 2 ac lead + 2 years for consolidation, supervisory and subordinate development experience.

2nd SQUADRON Same type :
6 months to stablise + 1½ years as a Medium Level supervisor.

Different Type/ASF — 1 to 1½ years to consolidate with the remainder 1½ years as a Supervisor/Buddy.

With such a profile, one could hope for a positive cascading effect starting from improved QFI performance in FIS, more mature and focused QFIs with prior experience in close supervision and subordinate development, better trained cadets and, of course, improved flight safety.

Another method of giving teeth to the buddy and ML supervisor is to involve them in a Junior Leadership Programme at the Command level, which focuses on both leadership, motivational issues and flying/flight safety aspects. The programme could be divided into two phases of 15 days each. The first phase could be conducted as a joint package for two weeks, which gets together officers from all branches, brainstorming and discussing all issues that have a direct or indirect bearing on flight safety. Some focal issues could be:

- How each branch can contribute to flight safety
- Leadership, teamwork and synergy
- Contentious issues that exist in flying bases
- A reorientation on SOPs, standing orders, and restrictions related to Op with specific emphasis on flight safety
- Discussion of case studies
- Human and hygiene factors

An intensive flying capsule could follow this for 1–2 weeks involving aircrew, ATCOs and radar controllers at a few type-specific locations, with a laid-down programme that revolves around supervision, mentoring and accident prevention. The aim of the programme would be to improve flight safety in the field by enhancing leadership skill and teamwork amongst officers in the 4–8 year bracket of all branches.

Conclusion

The time is not far when the IAF will be expected to restructure and become leaner and meaner. Intake of short-service commissioned officers may increase, and for the organization to exploit their potential fully there is a need to exhort officers from the 4–10 years bracket to consolidate quickly in their disciplines and assume the role of the vital middle link that is missing today. In doing so, flight safety is bound to improve significantly.

ETHICS AND VALUES IN
MILITARY LEADERSHIP

V alues are the basic building blocks of a warrior's character. They help warriors judge what is right or wrong in any situation. They form the very identity of

the Armed Forces, the solid rock on which everything else stands, especially in combat. They are the glue that binds together the members of a noble profession.

In our relentless quest for success, recognition and even fame, we in the military seem to have become obsessed with 'Doing a Thing Right' rather that

This paper is an adaptation of an earlier article by the author on a similar subject that was published in the **Air Power Journal** in 2006 and was presented at an Out Reach Air Power Seminar at The Air Force Academy, Hyderabad.

'Doing the Right Thing'. Intense competition to climb the 'Pyramid' and numerous environmental compulsions, deadlines and pressures has resulted in ethics, values and principles falling by the wayside. Tenure-based performance has led to commanders across the board resorting to methods and styles of leadership that ensure quick results and short-term gains as against the crying need of the hour, which demands visionary leadership and solid institution building. Over the last 10 years or so we have been reading extensively about ethics and values in corporate governance — Infosys and Tatas are now household names! Why is it that the Indian armed forces are no longer seen as bastions of ethical and value-based leadership? During the earlier days of the Indian Air Force, nobody really talked about values and ethics because it was ingrained in almost every action that was done or every word that was written or spoken. Today, the time has come to start laying the foundation of an ethical and value-based leadership once again, also we run the danger of having the very structure of our house destroyed. Before proceeding further, we need to ask ourselves two basic questions and answer them as honestly as we can.

- Are we facing a crisis of leadership, not in terms of performance and results, but in terms of ethics and values?
- If we are genuinely concerned, what is the way forward? Is there a need to widely institutionalize the teaching of values and ethics in military institutions of learning?

The bottom line of course, is to first recognize the need for ethical and value-based military leadership and to reaffirm its importance in projecting the armed forces as an instrument of credible national power. Only then can we shake off the cocooned feeling that all is right and start reflecting at all levels as to what needs to be done to restore the pride, élan and impeccable pedigree of the armed forces.

Core Definition of Ethics and Values

There is no better place to start than at the Core definition of ethics and values. Ethics as defined by the Concise Oxford Dictionary is 'the science of morals', moral principles and rules of conduct. It relates to what is honourable, or the morally correct, or the study of both right and wrong. Some questions that immediately spring up when one looks at the bare definition are: Where do these morals come from? What is their source and can we use them as a template for both our professional and personal conduct at all times? Only when these questions are answered convincingly will a military leader apply them to all facets of his leadership, be it during peace or war. Ethics owes its origin to the great Greek philosophers Plato, Socrates and Aristotle, and is a literal translation of the word 'ethos', which means habitual or customary conduct. To Aristotle,[1] ethics meant the study of excellence in the virtues of character. Closer home, the *Bhagavad Gita* propounded the concept of 'Dharma' or 'righteousness' or doing one's duty, be it in peace or in the battlefield.[2] With the advent of Christianity, the moral aspects of what the Church considered right or wrong crept into military ethics. The Chinese have also contributed in full measure in the area of what military leaders should and should not do, through the teachings of Confucius and Tsun Zu. From all these philosophical musings and moral codes laid down by emerging and established religions and philosophers emerged a set of **rules of conduct** that was **honourable**. If one looks at the two phrases underlined, in ancient times these were applicable only in two main activities, viz. sports and warfare. These Rules of Conduct and Honour Code have stood the test of time and have formed the foundation for the emergence of a number of value systems. Truth, Justice, Equality, Integrity and Courage are amongst the key examples of military ethics.

What then are values? Falling back again on the Concise Oxford Dictionary, it means one's principles or standard, one's judgment of what is valuable or important in life. It relates to 'attaching significance or 'regarding highly'. From the definition, what emerges clearly is the fact that values are personal benchmarks that are greatly influenced by parents, teachers, mentors, peers, superiors and of course, the environment. Mark the world environment because today the environment, more than anything else, has become the scapegoat for decaying values. If one were to explain very simply to young military officers and men, one could say that ethics is a broad, strong and inviolable framework that comprises a few rules of military and personal conduct in which you fit in values that are needed and situational based, as spelt out from time to time by the top leadership. Integrity comes from a Latin word that means 'entire' and 'whole'. In relation to professional conduct, we define integrity as 'uncompromised values', i.e. professionalism is behaviour aligned with uncompromised values. To be consistently professionally effective requires balancing passion, vision, and action, with integrity and aligning these elements each step along the way. Integrity according to many purists is the only way out and encompasses all known ingredients of

---

1   Aristotle, *Nichomachean Ethics*, Indianapolis Bobbs-Merril 1985.
2   Gen. (Retd.) Shankar Roy Chowdhary, *Culture and Military Ethics*, Ramakrishna Math-Vedanta Kesari.

leadership. In short, integrity is uncompromising; it is neither dictated by environmental, nor by organizational compulsions.

Historical Evolution and Decay of Military Ethics and Values

Images of the great warrior Arjun being given a treatise on morals, ethics and *values* on the battlefield by Lord Krishna are vivid in every Indian's mind. Should he decimate the revered teachers who had taught him every skill they knew, or the very warrior cousins he had grown up with? That was when Lord Krishna stepped in with his Divine justification of Dharma Yudha or the Righteous War, a war he urged Arjun to fight with a clear conscience because it was the right thing to do.[3] Homer's heroes from the *Illiad* and the *Odyssey* fought each other at Troy over a moral violation of ethics. Battlefield ethics of fighting equals and returning the bodies of slain warriors indicated the existence of an honour code.[4] The Roman Empire fell because of a progressive decay in morals and ethics, which blinded successive emperors from differentiating between what was right and wrong. They ordered the military to plunder destroy and rape and the military blindly obeyed till the rage of the common man pulled the Empire down. The birth of Christianity and Islam exerted renewed pressure on the military leadership, forcing them to throw aside classical military ethics and values like honour, integrity, courage and honesty in order to spread religion. The Industrial Revolution and its fallout of colonisation did have its share of unscrupulous and unethical conquests of natives, but at the same time it laid the foundation for the emergence of a world wide similarity in military leadership, as practised by the British and the French. Ethics and values as practised by British stalwarts like the Duke of Wellington, who once said, "The battle of Waterloo was once the playing field of Eton", indicated that good military leadership could not be acquired in a matter of days or weeks but accrued from years of value-based grooming and learning.

While military ethics has remained almost static for thousands of years, military values have undergone many transformations. Historically, military leaders have always struggled to cope with political or nationalist directives and modern military values owe their origin to the emergence of the Nation State and the rapid proliferation of military technology. World War II saw the success of Generals like Rommel and Slim, who occupied the moral and ethical high ground and still won. Rommel always struggled to come to terms with Nazi Germany, yet managed to carve an exemplary niche for himself amidst the moral degradation that was to ultimately cause the collapse of Nazi Germany. It

---

3   Ibid.
4   Aristotle, *Nichomachean Ethics.*

also saw the emergence of politically savvy Generals like Eisenhower who were tactically sound, yet malleable and flexible. Then came Korea and Vietnam wherein a nation's military leadership completely succumbed to political manipulation. The aftermath of the Vietnam War saw a complete re-appraisal of military leadership in the US Armed forces. A grass root drive was initiated to restore the faith of a nation in its military leadership and of the men in uniform in their leaders.

Closer home, General Thimayya's resistance to the 'Forward Policy' and Defence Minister Krishna Menon's highhanded treatment of senior military officers was based on the need to preserve the honour of the armed forces. It is another matter, however that the ill-fated forward policy was ultimately implemented, leading to the 1962 China debacle which brought into focus the need to reinforce ethics and values that were severely compromised during the conflict in the Indian Army. General Manekshaw epitomized all that was best in military values and ethics when he refused to cow down to political diktats and move into Bangladesh prematurely. This he did primarily out of a fierce sense of loyalty to the men and officers he commanded and with the courage of conviction to say that the Indian Army was not ready to move into Bangladesh for a variety of environmental reasons. To a large extent, the success of the coalition forces during 'Op Desert Storm' was due to focused, ethical and value-based military leadership as displayed by both General Shwartzkopf and General Horner. The same cannot be said of the recent war in Iraq were the media has exposed the blatant aberration in military values and ethics by the US and British soldiers in the absence of any strong value-based leadership at the top.[5] History is replete with examples of both upholding what are best in military ethics and values and what are worst. It is for practitioners of this profession to dig into history and make a choice.

Pressure on Military Leadership

The changing nature of warfare and expansion of national interests well beyond geographical boundaries have placed fresh challenges on military leadership. Terrorism, insurgencies and ethnic warfare have seen the most brutal and horrifying excesses in Bosnia, Chechnya and Rwanda. The proliferation of democracy has also placed fresh demands on military leadership in terms of compliance and taking orders from political masters. Materialism and economic progress have exerted their own pressures on the

---

5   Human Rights Watch Report 2004, *The Road to Abu Gharib.*

moderately paid practitioners of the military profession. Intense media scrutiny has also resulted in many leadership aberrations being made public, forcing the military leadership to increasingly look inwards and focus on ethics and values. There has always existed a pyramidal structure in the armed forces; competition has always been intense and soldiers in the past have retired or exited from service gracefully and with minimum fuss. This was mainly due to two reasons. First, there was very little transparency in the assessment and promotion system and second, the 'honour' code was so strongly ingrained in officers that aberrations were kept inhouse, to preserve the 'izzat' of the defence services and not wash dirty linen in public. Today, things are completely different. Military leaders do not want to retire young because of economic and resettlement uncertainties. There is, at times, an intense desire in many leaders whose ambition far exceeds their ability to rise in rank by 'hook or by crook'. In this race up the ladder, ethics, values and principles are the first casualties. Increasing transparency has now come into play and leaders who feel they have been denied a rightful place in the sun have started taking the legal route to redress their grievances, bringing issues of fairplay, ethics and values into the limelight.

Equally troublesome are perplexing questions faced by commanders in anti-terrorist, Internal Security and Counter Insurgency duties where the divide between right and wrong is wafer-thin. How does one adhere to the *Principle of Jus ad Bellum*, which lays down what constitutes a just cause for a decision to wage war and *Jus in Bello*,which decides who should be immune from direct and intentional attacks in war? When targeting enemy military forces, how should officers and soldiers weigh force protection against civilian casualties?[6] How do you teach your men and officers to retain their sense of balance in the face of brutal, unscrupulous and fanatic insurgents and terrorists who exploit the land and local people to their advantage, even using them as human shields? With rapidly changing social norms and increasing permissiveness in society, marital discord and extra-marital liaisons amongst men and women in uniform is on the increase. How do military leaders cope with such changes? AIDS is another challenge in our search for a new set of ethics and values for the military. How do we, as military leaders, cope with these problems and instill in our officers and men a set of ethics that is constant and values that combine progressive thought and conservative tradition with the aim of making the military leader stand out in comparison to business and political leaders as guardians of a free and progressive democracy?

---

6   Dr David L Perry, Strategic Leadership Course, US Army War College, 2005.

Different Perspectives on Values and Ethics

The aftermath of the Vietnam War and public outcry against declining morals, values and ethics forced the US armed forces to look inward and institutionalize the ethics and values that were expected of men and women in uniform. In the mid 1990s the US army formally listed its seven values[7] as:

- Loyalty
- Duty
- Respect
- Selfless service
- Honour
- Integrity
- Personal courage
- Character.

The USAF concised it to just three Core values,[8] viz:

- Integrity first
- Service before self
- Excellence in all we do.

Some of the issues that merit close attention and are universally relevant are discussed below. These traits have been particularly singled out as they are perceived to be important in the context of the Indian armed forces too.

- **Loyalty:** Loyalty should not be confused with blind obedience to illegal or unethical orders. Leaders must follow their conscience when giving orders and subordinates must exercise their judgment when the orders are unethical and violate the laid-down values. As long as leaders and subordinates understand that loyalty is first to the organization, its values and principles and not to the individual, the dividing line between loyalty and sycophancy would be clearly defined.
- **Respect:** A good leader must always respect individuals, whether senior or junior. He must honour their status, value their opinion and accept inputs humbly for whatever they are worth. Individuality and self-esteem must be respected, as that will foster mutual respect, something that is imperative for

---

7   Seven Army Values,US Army Field Manual 22-100.
8   USAF — Little Blue Book.

value-based teamwork. It is very common to confuse respect and subservience. While respect is an affirmation of mutual or one-sided affirmation of professional capability or personal standards, subservience is 'blind respect' that is based on fear, greed and ambition.

- **Integrity:** Integrity of thought and action is integral to good military leadership. A person of integrity does not change moral principles when they become unpopular or inconvenient. Broadly speaking, this means adherence to moral and ethical standards. Integrity is all-encompassing and includes both moral and physical courage, honesty, propriety, accountability and justice. A look at the USAF values indicates that excellence is important, but it is number three on the list. What can be deduced from this? It is a realization that if one concentrates on the means and the methods, keeping the good of the organisation or your immediate environment in mind, excellence will automatically follow.

The Chinese Model

The simplest articulation of ethics and values for the military can be traced back to the early days of Mao and the Long March. In its early days, the PLA formulated its three Main Rules of Discipline and Eight Points for Attention, which laid down ethical rules of conduct for its personnel.[9] It reflected a grass root approach and has stood the test of time. Some of the prominent ones are:

- Do not take a single piece of thread from the masses.
- Speak politely.
- Pay fairly for what you buy.
- Return everything you borrow.
- Pay for anything you damage.
- Do not hit or swear at people.
- Do not damage crops.

Erosion of Ethics and Values in the Indian Armed Forces

Ethics and value systems in the Indian armed forces have never been institutionalized. Rather, we have rather relied on tradition and hand-me-downs to inculcate ethics and values in our officers and troops. The armed forces have lived and operated in isolation all these years, admired from a distance by both

---

9   Chinese White Paper on Defence, PRC State Council Information. Office, December 2004.

the common people and the political establishment. Ethical misdemeanours were more often than not viewed as mere aberrations and not systemic faults and swept under the carpet after symbolic courts of inquiries or even court martials. Institutional concern was not very apparent as the overall quality of military leadership was considered to be very high and comparable to the best in the world. Things started changing in the 1990s because of geopolitical and environmental changes. The major factors that have accelerated the erosion of ethics and values in the Indian armed forces are:

- Rapid economic growth and growing disparity in incomes between the military and other professions
- Increased involvement of the armed forces in internal security duties without adequate institutionalized sensitization
- Increased involvement in anti-terrorist operations and the associated dilemmas of Force Protection vs Non Combatant immunity, collateral damage and civilian casualties
- Enhanced civil-military, para-military liaison and increase in exposure of men in uniform to various forms of corruption
- Poor resettlement opportunities for officers and men who superannuate early in life
- Changed priorities of the younger generation and absence of enough 'role models', coupled with reluctance on the part of senior officers to assume serious mentoring roles
- Lack of any serious institutionalized training in ethics and value-based leadership for officers and men
- Intense media scrutiny of matters relating to the military
- Closed assessment system and absence of a fair inhouse redressal system, which forces military personnel to go to court and tarnish the image of the armed forces.
- Changing morality of personal relationships in society.

The Way Forward

The only way forward is to first recognize the fact that ethics and values in the armed forces in general are being routinely compromised. The feeling 'If you get away with it then it does not matter if it was right or wrong' and that it 'pays to be a winner' is widely prevalent and accepted. The next step is to adopt a bottom–up approach in inculcating ethics and values in both officers and other ranks. Presently, there is no institutionalized sensitization to the importance of ethics and values in good military leadership. Along with military history why can we not introduce ethics and values as part of the curriculum at the NDA and the Air Force Academy as part of a character building and training programme? Why can't we include the study of ethics and values from an even younger age at our Sainik schools and institutions like RIMC? We have also seen a top–down approach in which senior officers articulate their views and concerns on values, ethics and leadership and expect the younger generation to accept them without understanding them or being convinced about the 'payoffs' of ethical and value-based leadership. Instead, why don't we start at the very bottom of the pyramid? Do we really believe that a few leadership capsules conducted by institutions like the College of Defence Management and the CLABS (Centre for leadership and Behavioural Studies) at the College of Air Warfare are likely to inculcate good leadership skills. Yes! It is a good beginning, but it should be accompanied by a grass root drive to inculcate the ability to differentiate right from wrong. A cleared databank of ethical misdemeaneours over the years must be created and shared periodically along with the action taken by the three services in order to drive home the point that no compromise is acceptable as far as ethics and values are concerned. A reduction in the involvement of the armed forces in internal security duties is an inescapable imperative as adhering to the core profession of arms. This would make it easier to adhere to core values and ethics of the military profession and insulate various rungs of military leadership from the risks, temptations and pressures associated with internal security duties. Resettlement and parallel absorption in the public and private sector of retired officers and men or veterans as they are now called, is very vital in keeping relatively young military leaders secure about their future. Compromising ethics and moral values in order to secure an uncertain future is one troubling issue that needs to be addressed on priority. Mentoring in the armed forces is becoming a lost art that has to be revived if we are to pass on ethics, values and traditions to the younger generation. Middle-ranking and senior officers are, at times, so busy furthering their own careers that they see little value in investing time and intellect on the younger generation, who in turn are getting used to 'quick-fix' solutions and becoming increasingly reluctant to take the difficult path of doing the 'right thing'.

Sceptics may say that the study of ethics and values is of no use as it carries little meaning in the 'heat of combat operations'. Nothing can be further from the truth. It is only when you continuously reflect on good ethics and values, that you will arrive at the correct decision in battle or under pressure. So, the Mantra should be: Catch them young and inculcate in them the ability to quickly differentiate between right and wrong so that when the going gets tough, a military leader seldom takes the easy way out.

Values for the Modern Military Leader

Moral values and ethics can either be enforced by law or ensured by creating an environment of fear, the likes of which existed behind the Iron Curtain. Sadly, these methods have never stood the test of time and crumble in the face of adversity or 'when no one is looking'. Personal conviction[10] is the only way to ensure sustenance of any framework that exists for ethical conduct in the armed forces. As alluded to earlier, it is important to clearly establish an ethical framework for our men and officers, which helps them distinguish the right from wrong from a very early stage of their military careers. This can be termed as Core Ethics and could include inviolable attributes like Integrity, Honesty, Responsibility, Accountability, Justice, Trust and Courage. It is not enough to articulate these in a document or doctrine or a 'White Paper', but necessary to actually to go down to the nurseries of military education and teach our young cadets and officers with examples from history, relating them to their present lives. Having established a basic framework, it is for the leadership to spell out the values that fit into the framework, and these values would form the building blocks of a strong and enduring organization. Leadership has two components, viz. technical expertise and moral authority. Technical expertise is the ability and knowledge necessary to do what must be done to accomplish the desired objective. Moral authority is knowledge of and concern for what is best for those who follow you. Some of the values that may be considered as age-old values, and some have emerged as a result of our changing times. A sample of these attributes is given below. These values should be able to guide and motivate our military leaders to realize both organisational and personal goals.

- Professional excellence
- Self-confidence
- Flexibility of thought and action
- Decision-making ability
- Technology orientation
- Intellectual ability
- Multi-skilling ability

Ethical and Value Imperatives for Senior Military Leadership

To avoid unnecessary clutter, it is also important to lay down certain imperatives

---

10   Maj. Gen. Jerry E. White, Personal Ethics vs Professional Ethics, *Air Power Journal*, Summer 1996, pp 30–34.

for Senior Military Leadership, as the consequences of their actions can be far reaching. The additional burden of Command puts senior military leaders in the cynosure of not only the eyes of the men they lead, but in the eyes of millions of their countrymen, thanks to the increasingly transparent, even prying media. Let us acknowledge that the pressures on them are tremendous. Apart from diverse, invisible and often unscrupulous opponents in battle, they also have to cope with the chronic stress of modern-day living, which permeates from their own personal lives to the lives of the men under their command as well as their families. The highly regimented, rule-bound, fast-moving and competitive work environment may lead to feelings of alienation, inadequacy, powerlessness and worry about basic survivals in the rat race. In such a situation, unless a leader is equipped with all the basic core values and ethics and reinforced with years of experience and wisdom, the chances of taking unethical or wrong decisions are very high. This was clearly evident in the recent cases of prisoner abuse at Guantanamo Bay and Abu Gharib where senior coalition leaders are said to have tacitly approved of the debasing torture of legitimate POWs[11].

- **Credibility and Trust** Credibility and trust go hand-in-hand. Spell out to your subordinates clearly what you expect of them. Share your vision with them and live your values as you preach them[12]. Do that and you will win their trust and their efforts. The maxim of practice what you preach and only preach what you can practice is extremely important to win the trust and loyalty of increasingly discerning, aware and intelligent subordinates.
- **Control of the environment** Control of the environment is important to do the Right Thing. Let the environment control you and you will fall prey to the pressure it exerts on you. Control of the environment is only possible if a military leader is professionally sound, politically aware and environmentally sensitive. This would ensure a proactive approach towards ensuring a harmonius politico-military relationship, and that the prestige and honour of the armed forces is maintained at a time when the bureaucracy, police and para-military forces are growing increasingly assertive.
- **Risk Vs Ethics and Duty Vs Conscience Dilemmas** Understanding the risk vs ethics and duty vs conscience dilemmas are very important for military leaders at all levels. Service in the armed forces is risky. Risk takers are more prone to making mistakes and getting into trouble. If you crucify honest mistakes, it will lead to a loss of values like initiative and courage. So you need to institute

---

11   Ibid. no 5.
12   Jack Ward Thomas, Chief USDA Forest Service, Sociey of American Foresters Convention, Portland Maine, November 1995.

measures to educate these risk takers on the moral and ethical dimension of their actions so that an element of caution creeps into the risk, making it a trifle more balanced. It is a tough call and has to be honestly addressed. History is again littered with generals having to go into battle with a 'sinking feeling' that the higher decision, though not morally the right one, was probably the only decision left in the overall national interest. *Operation Bluestar* and *Operation Pawan* in Sri Lanka are two classic examples wherein the Indian armed forces placed duty above everything else, suffered heavy casualties, but came out with their heads held high because of a stable and focused leadership. More recently, this issue has assumed fresh significance with a number of retired US generals including Gen. Anthony Zinni and General Shinseki coming out with scathing attacks against Donald Rumsfield for riding roughshod over sane professional military advice and going into Iraq in 'cowboy style' with inadequate troops for peace enforcement and peacekeeping. The outburst, it appears, is a long pent-up conflict between duty and conscience, something that gets extremely difficult for senior military leaders to resolve in such situations. In the final analysis it will be inner strength that is bolstered by strong ethics and values that will show the way.

- Developing your subordinates for tough and varied combat conditions is another aspect of today's fluid battlefield environment. Training them for instinctive decision making under pressure will only happen if they are capable of independent thought and action of doing the Right Thing at the Right Time.

- Senior military leaders like winners, but they must realize that all winners don't do the Right Thing. Right values are neither safe, easy or advantageous. Practitioners of right ethics and values often lose, but they still go ahead and lose because they defend the values that have been ingrained in them[13].

- Complex decision making at senior levels also involves the dilemma of right vs right. How do you resolve an issue that pits truth vs loyalty or the individual vs the team or short-term gains vs long-term ones? Do you stick to a rule-based solution or a 'care'-based one, or do you decide where the greatest good for maximum people is achieved?

- **Transformational Leadership** Transformational leaders are those who seek, by means of moral example, to persuade followers to adopt a goal that is in the best interest of the service. Example is not the main thing; it is the only thing. The transformational leader, therefore, is neither morally or intellectually arrogant because his success does not depend upon merely

13   Norman Shwarzkopf, 'Ethical Leadership in the 21st Century', Talk at the Institute for National Leadership, February 2004.

reaching a certain objective, but depends upon convincing his followers that the goal is worthwhile. It is the goal of the transformational military leader to create a morally courageous, physically tough and technically proficient force that will to continue to realize its objectives in the future, even when the present leader is no longer present[14]. 'We', not 'I' is the hallmark of such leadership.

- **Humanity** Combat, peacekeeping and peace enforcement operations run the risk of failure despite all the training, contingency planning and tactical brilliance, and at times the only intangible element that propels the final push that transforms defeat into victory is a leader's ability to call on hidden reserves of endurance and willpower in the men he commands. Invariably, this is possible only if a leader is humane, leads from the front and has a genuine 'feel' for the troops he commands.
- **Professional and Personal Ethics** Unlike the ongoing debate that is raging in 'civvy street and the corporate sector' on the need to separate professional ethics and conduct from personal conduct and ethics, military leaders have no such choice. Their lives are so entwined with those of their subordinates that every action of theirs is a mirror for others to emulate, hence the crying need for consistent ethical and moral standards, both at work and at home[15].

The Paradox of Modern Combat

The enemy our parents and grandparents faced wore a different uniform to theirs, but had aims and, by and large, conduct that they could understand. The enemy fought much as we fought; his forces were structured much the same way. For the most part, they accepted the same conventions. Today's most dangerous, global enemy, the terrorist[16], does not.

We face an adversary:

- Who revels in mass murder
- Who sets out to cause the greatest pain it can to innocent people
- Who is entirely unconstrained by any law
- Who sees all civilians, including women and children not as non-combatants but as easy targets
- Who sees terror as a key part of its arsenal
- Who both glorifies and operates suicide bombers.

---

14   Ibid, n. 12.
15   Ibid, n. 11.
16   And the same is true of many protagonists in 'new', especially asymmetric, wars.

He is an enemy unfettered by any sense of morality [17].

Sustained engagement with such a 'different' enemy not only challenges the moral sureties expected by the regular — the combatant/non-combatant distinction, lawful/non-lawful and so on — but it may lead to frustration: a temptation to hit out at what he can. This is almost certainly the principal explanation for the more numerous allegations of wrongful behaviour by regular soldiers in asymmetric than in conventional conflict.

Emotional Intelligence — Ethics and Values

One of the emerging imperatives for the modern military leader is Emotional Intelligence (EI). Without sticking to traditional definitions, EI is a composite character trait that amalgamates native intelligence, logical reasoning and intrinsic military ability with a sound collection of institutional ethics and values. This then becomes a potent force multiplier when it comes to decision-making. If one looks at some of the articulated ingredients of EI,[18] like emotional self-awareness, transparency, adaptability, empathy, team work, conflict management, inspirational leadership and a sense of service; strong ethics and values, ability to resolve moral dilemmas and differentiating between right and wrong are at the forefront of this strong reservoir of EI.

Case Study

In June 2005, Col. Ted Westhusing, a 44-year-old leading military ethicist, scholar and full Professor at West Point, was found dead in Baghdad with a single gunshot wound to the head. The army concluded that he had committed suicide with his service pistol. He was, at that time, the highest-ranking service officer to die in Iraq. A note found in his trailer seemed to offer some clues as it read: HOW IS HONOUR POSSIBLE IN A WAR LIKE IRAQ! Colonel Westhusing had volunteered to serve in Iraq because he was upset with reports of unethical practices in Iraq and wanted to try and help in stemming the rot. It was only a matter of time before he is reported to have received a complaint that a private security company had cheated the Government and committed human rights violations. He reportedly confronted the contractor and conveyed his concerns

---

17   John Reid, Speech at King's College, London, 20 February 2006. Online at http://www.mod.uk/ DefenceInternet/DefenceNews/DefencePolicyAndBusiness/WeMustBeSlowerToCondemnAndQuicke rToUnderstandTheForcesJohnReid.htm

18   Lt. Col. Sharon Latour & Lt. Gen. Brad Hosmer USAF (Retd) Emotional Intelligence: Implications for USAF Leaders-Air Command & Staff College Coursebook on Leadership.

to superiors who launched an investigation. In an emotional email to his family he seemed very upset that traditional military values such as honour, duty and country had been replaced by profit motives where the military had come to rely on contractors for jobs once done by the military. His family will never know whether Colonel Westhusing actually committed suicide because he was depressed or was done in by the contractors.[19]

Conclusion

Stephen Covey, in his book *The Seven Habits of Highly Effective People* clearly mentions that managers are trained to do a thing right and leaders do the right thing. The military needs leaders because good leaders almost always turn out to be good managers, whatever their style may be. As far as the Indian armed forces are concerned, it would augur well to see the signs emerging from Iraq and the conduct of the occupying coalition forces. The saying' 'fore-warned is forearmed' rings true in the case of enhanced awareness of the need for ethical and value based military leadership. Education and awareness programmes are vital for integrating these values in doctrine and training plans. Ethics is never dispensable. It is an integral part of human survival. But in the 21st century, such survival will be more complicated and precarious than ever before, and the ethics required of us must be correspondingly sophisticated. Finally, ethics is absolutely necessary to tackle the pressure of the truth, occupy the moral high ground and re-enforce the position of the military as the vanguard of a nation's leadership.

> *To educate a man in mind and not morals is to*
> *educate a menace to society.*
>
> **Theodore Roosevelt**

---

19   Who Killed Col Ted Westhusing? Blogs at www.moreaples@hotmail.com

AIR POWER AND GEOPOLITICS SECTION

A SCHOLAR SOLDIER IS NOT A CONTRADICTION. HE IS, IN FACT, A PRODUCT OF OUR CHANGING TIMES. THE MORE A SOLDIER READS, THE FURTHER HE WOULD STAY AHEAD OF POTENTIAL ADVERSARIES, ESPECIALLY IN TIMES LIKE THESE WHEN ADVERSARIES ARE ALMOST INVISIBLE. THE OLD ADAGE 'THE PEN IS MIGHTIER THAN THE SWORD' DOES NOT HOLD TRUE FOR MEN IN UNIFORM. IN FACT, FOR US SOLDIERS, THE PEN, THE INTELLECT AND THE SWORD, WHEN WIELDED TOGETHER, MAKE A DEADLY AND UNBEATABLE COMBINATION.

HOW WE NEED TO THINK, TRAIN AND FIGHT IN THE COMING YEARS

Real exploitation of air power's potential can only come through making assumptions that it can do something we thought it couldn't do. . . . We must start our thinking by assuming we can do everything with air power, not by assuming that it can only do what it did in the past.

-Col John Warden

THE STRATEGIC ROLE OF AIR POWER

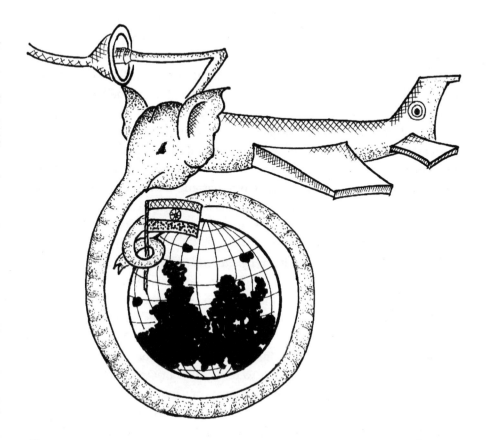

Abstract

*T*he application of airpower to further a nation's strategic objectives has gained momentum over the last few years, ever since it has been used with telling effect in Operation Desert Storm, over Kosovo and during Operation Iraqi Freedom. Notwithstanding the tremendous asymmetry displayed in these conflicts, the advent of sensors that provide accurate target intelligence, coupled with Precision-Guided Munitions, has led to 'effects-based operations' gaining predominance in speedy conflict resolution, with minimum attrition and collateral damage. The IAF is in the midst of a radical change in mindset and reorientation of its force structure so that it is capable of conducting 'parallel' warfare and influencing operations at the tactical, operational and strategic levels. It is in the light of these developments that there is a need to 'think, train and fight' with a 'strategic' focus.

This article is a prize-winning article, which was published in the Oct-Dec 2006 edition of *Air Power Journal*.

Conceptual Development

The use of airpower to further a nation's strategic aims and objectives has come a long way since the pounding of Nazi Germany's ball-bearing factories on the Rhine by Allied Bombers and the obliteration of Hiroshima and Nagasaki, both of which had a significant bearing on the outcome of World War II. Versions of WW II vintage bombers like the B-17, B-24 in the 1940s, the B-52, in the 1950s and their Russian counterparts like the TU-126 in the 1960s were modified to carry nuclear missiles and warheads. This added a new dimension to strategic air power, that of deterrence.[20] The application of air power to further strategic objectives and engage in coercive diplomacy has seen tremendous success over the last 40 years barring an odd failure. Without constantly harping on the contribution of the strategic application of airpower at Hiroshima and Nagasaki as the prime catalyst for the surrender of Japan, numerous examples that cut across intensities of conflicts exist to push the case for a re-appraisal of the swift benefits of the Strategic Air Campaign. Whether it was *Operation Linebacker I* and *II*[21] that allowed the US to draw the Viet Cong back to the negotiating table in 1971-1972, or the surgical strikes on Arab airfields by the Israelis in 1967, target selection was the key to the achievement of strategic objectives. As against this, poor target selection during *Operation Rolling Thunder* from 1965 to 1968 led to its total failure. The strategy of targeting The Ho Chi Minh Trail and centres of population in North Vietnam proved to be blunders that were rectified in *Operation Linebacker II*, where only military and infrastructure elements of national power were targeted.[22]

Next came the redefinition of platforms to prosecute the strategic air campaign and the consequent understanding that the strategic air campaign was better focussed when one looked at the 'effect' of destruction on the ability or will of a nation to wage war rather than the target and platform itself. The choice of attack platforms today also represents a radical shift from the Strategic Bomber concept. Role reversal of strategic and tactical aircraft commenced in Vietnam where B-52s carried out missions in support of ground operations while F-4s and F-105s flew against strategic interdiction targets deep inside North Vietnam. Years later eight F-16s, primarily considered in the USAF and the Israeli Air Force as tactical platforms, destroyed the Iraqi nuclear reactor at Osirak in what was considered a classic strategic strike.[23] The final

---

20   Air Chief Marshal Sir Michael Knight, 'Strategic Offensive Air Operations', Brasseys Airpower Series, 1989, pp. 48–60.

21   Duncan Bell, The Seductive Promise of Air Power-Strategic Coercion in Vietnam (and beyond?), Centre for International Studies, Cambridge University, *Air Power Review*, Summer 2000 Vol. 3. Issue 2.

22   Ibid.

23   Mark J. Conversino, 'The Changed Nature of Strategic Air Attack', *Parameters*, Winter 1997-98 pp. 28–41.

fillip to the case for strategic airpower is, without doubt, the emergence of highly accurate PGMs coupled with real-time intelligence and 'just in time targeting', which allows a nation to exert its will on another without committing ground forces and paving the way for negotiated settlement to conflicts without unnecessary collateral damage and loss of life. A classic example of this redefinition, which may not be palatable to the Counter Air purists, would be the destruction of Arab aircraft on the ground in 1967 during the classic Counter Air Campaign launched by the Israeli Air Force. Were not the effects 'strategic' in terms of breaking the Arab coalition's ability and will to fight? Enough has been articulated over the years on the spectacular success of the Coalition Air Forces in *Operation Desert Storm* where an 'effects'-based Strategic Air Campaign conceived by Colonel John Warden and executed by Lt General Chuck Horner achieved President Bush's 'Strategic Objective' of driving Iraq out of Kuwait with minimum attrition.[24] If one were to pinpoint one failure of the use of Strategic Air Power in recent years, it was the failure of the USAF to eliminate Osama-Bin-Laden and the top Taliban leadership, which was one of the main strategic objectives of *Operation Enduring Freedom*. If mass, tonnage, widespread area bombing due to lack of hard intelligence, collateral damage and indiscriminate loss of life were the prime characteristics of the Strategic Air Campaign of yesteryears, stealth, precision, intense shock effect and speedy capitulation of the enemy along with the achievement of objectives is the result of the 21st-century strategic air campaign.

Sceptics may say that the next few generations may not see a world war and that force structures of developing countries like India need to be focussed on waging local wars under hi-tech conditions, low-intensity conflicts and counter-insurgencies. They could not be farther from the truth as the coming years would see a struggle for strategic resources, strategic points and strategic markets, most of which could spread across the globe thousands of miles from a country's geographical boundaries. A threat to these assets would warrant speedy intervention, something that only air power could achieve. The case for further developing the IAF's strategic air capability in the coming years cannot but be over-emphasised in the light of India's emergence as a potential economic super power with global energy interests and markets. The need for swift, precise and decisive intervention in potential hotspots spread across continents can only be achieved by synergistic joint operations, with air power being used as a springboard or a launch-pad for further intervention by land and naval forces.

---

24   Richard T. Reynolds, Col. USAF, *Heart of the Storm*, Air University Press, Maxwell Air Force Base Alabama, January 1995.

Understanding Paralysis, Asymmetry, and Parallel Warfare

The three main objectives of any military campaign have always been coercion or intimidation, incapacitation or dismemberment and annihilation or destruction. These military objectives have always been focussed in the direction of achievement of a nation's geopolitical objectives in any dispute or conflict. Warfare in the 21st century is slowly moving towards keeping destruction or annihilation as a last resort in legitimate war-fighting scenarios. With this in focus, two air power theorists from the USAF, Colonels Warden and Boyd propounded path-breaking theories of paralysing the enemy by strategic application of air power.[25] While Boyd talks about paralysing the enemy psychologically and weakening his will to fight, Warden emphasizes the need to physically paralyse the adversary by attacking leadership, infrastructure, communication links and fielded forces as part of his now famous 'Five Ring Theory' based on Clausewitz's Centres of Gravity, which formed the heart of the air campaign in *Operation Desert Storm*. The cornerstone of this process is the high probability of pounding an enemy into submission without inflicting too many casualties, and reducing the intensity of contact battles by driving his leadership 'underground', blinding him, rendering his senses (eyes and ears) ineffective and destroying reserves and follow-on forces by carrying out 'deep precision strikes'. While the strategic air campaign that aims at paralysis is based on overwhelming asymmetry that US forces are likely to enjoy in any conflict scenario, it is important for policy and strategy planners in India too to understand the tremendous advantages of creating an asymmetry[26] vis-à-vis potential adversaries by building up a potent strategic air capability, built around technology, force multipliers and multi-theatre capability. At no stage is it considered that air power alone, that too the strategic air campaign alone can win a war by itself. What it certainly can do by applying the principles of asymmetry and paralysis, is to hasten the capitulation of an enemy by incapacitating him and reducing his military potential as mentioned earlier, rather than destroying him. All this can be done by air power simultaneously while providing support to the surface campaign by exploiting airpower's ability to conduct parallel warfare[27] at the tactical, operational and strategic levels. Building such an ability calls for acceptance of the need for asymmetry, change in mindset and significant alterations to asset allocation. In the Indian context,

---

25   John Boyd and John Warden, 'Air powers Quest for Strategic Paralysis', David S. Fadok, 'A thesis presented to the School for Advanced Air Power Studies', Maxwell AF Base, February 95.

26   Jasjit Singh, 'Strategic Framework for Defence Planners: Air Power in the 21st Century', Aero India 98 Seminar, 8–10 December 1998.

27   Rebecca Grant, 'The Redefinition of Strategic Air Power', *Air Force Magazine*, October 2003 pp. 33–38.

building up asymmetry cannot be restricted only to acquisition of technology, force multipliers and space-based sensors, as many would believe, in order to justify a 'leaner' air force. All the above need to be supplemented with numbers in terms of aircraft and platforms to be able to conduct parallel and asymmetric warfare on multiple fronts. This obviously calls for a strong case to 'beef up' the number of squadrons in the IAF from a projected 29 in 2008[28] to at least 40 squadrons by 2015.

Role Definition in the 21st Century

The emergence of invisible enemies, like terrorists and unconventional targets that revolve around material and human resources means that it will become increasingly difficult to classify the roles that strategic air assets would perform over the next few decades. If one were to identify the most critical characteristics of air power that would occupy centre-stage for the Indian Air Force in the years to come, they would be: flexibility, reach, fire power with precision and interoperability, with other characteristics like surprise and shock effect being age-old and time-tested corollary benefits. What is it about these four characteristics that makes them the focus of a study to define the roles of strategic air power for the IAF in the 21st century? The ability of a platform to effortlessly switch from a tactical to strategic role is an inescapable imperative as is its reach in performing 'interventionist' roles with appropriate combat support elements thousands of kilometres away from its launch base. Having reached its target, the platform must be able to neutralise the target with precision attacks and minimum collateral damage. The platforms and crew used for prosecuting the strategic air campaign must be able to operate in international airspace with varied sensors, and possibly with aircraft/aircrew of multinational task forces, especially in conflicts involving the UN/multinational forces. They also need to be well integrated with elements of the surface forces involved in strategic interventions so as to synergistically apply the principles of asymmetry in conflict resolution. Having broadly spelt out the framework, what then are the broad strategic roles and missions that the IAF can take on with a force structure that would revolve around ac like the SU-30 MKI, the MRCA, Mirage 2000, IL-78, IL-76 and the AWACS? While it would be very easy to ape the USAF and formulate a 'Strategic Air Campaign' and force that revolves around 'Centres of Gravity', nothing would be more divorced from the reality of the 'Indian situation'. Two major questions would need to be asked:

---

28   Sandeep Unnithan, 'Force in Free Fall', *India Today*, 10 April 06.

- Do we have the resources to prosecute such a campaign?
- Are we likely to be faced with an Iraq-like situation of a long-drawn sub-conventional war on foreign soil?

The answer would obviously be NO. This brings us back to a Strategic Intervention Capability revolving around economic progress, energy and people. Till now, the IAF has been seen as a predominantly tactical air force with limited deterrent capability. With the advent of platforms like the SU-30 MK-I, weapon systems like the Brahmos and force multipliers that include aerial refuelling platforms, UAVs and AWACS, there is a need to 'think big' and 'think far'. Conventional roles have to be replaced by roles that cater to the following scenarios:

- Power projection role
- Strategic intervention
- Proactive strikes and elimination of threats
- Humanitarian intervention
- Peace-keeping missions in a lead role
- Protection of energy and economic resources and island territories of Andaman & Nicobar and Lakshadweep
- Anti-terrorist and anti-hijacking operations
- Protection and evacuation of human resources
- Enforcement of 'No Fly Zones'.

In many of the scenarios and roles indicated above, while the Navy and Army would continue to form key components of a Joint Task Force, it is air power that would be used to intervene at short notice. Even when it comes to humanitarian intervention, the recent tsunami highlighted the speed and responsiveness of air power as also the need for additional resources in terms of heavy-lift helicopters and transport aircraft for disaster relief operations.

Targeting for Strategic Air Strikes

Targeting philosophy too has changed significantly over the years, dictated mainly by the nature and duration of wars, capability of platforms, accuracy of munitions and quality of intelligence. The slow and sequential effect of Strategic Bombing during World War II, and to some extent during Vietnam, did contribute significantly to the final outcome owing to repetitive attacks. This involved thousands of sorties against the same target sets without looking at civilian casualties and collateral damage, the main aim being to systematically undermine the industrial capability and psychologically numb an adversary into submission. Closer home the surgical strike by IAF MiG-21s on the Governor General's residence in Dacca in December 1971, did make a significant dent in the morale of the East Pak leadership, which ultimately resulted in their capitulation only days later. Wars and conflicts in the 21st century will be short and swift, necessitating extremely quick and effective targeting without having to resort to repetitive attacks. Redundancy and recuperability of economic targets has also shifted focus on the types of targets that need to be neutralised to hasten the end of a conflict. Typical changes in target profiles over the years are indicated in Table1.1 below:

Table 1.1 Target Sets

World War II	The Gulf Wars of 1991 and 2003
Population centres	Enemy leadership
Industrial capability	C3I systems and sensors
Manufacturing centres	Fielded forces and reserves
Hydroelectric and power generation	Nuclear and WMD sites

As can be seen, the focus has shifted from people and economy to leadership and military capability.[29]Targeting for the strategic application of air power was also totally redefined during *Operations Desert Shield, Desert Storm* and *Allied Force over Kosovo,* with significant refinements during *Operation Enduring Freedom* in Afghanistan and *Operation Iraqi Freedom* in 2003. As against a fairly rigid set of targets that were defined by perceived centres of gravity and folded into a largely individualistic strategic air campaign in 1991, the much publicized 'Shock and Awe' combined arms campaign of the 2003 Iraq war saw a number of strategic targets being engaged simultaneously by platforms as varied as classical strategic platforms like the B-2 bomber to purely tactical platforms like the F-16 and Predator UAVs armed with PGMs and a wide variety of 'Smart Weapons'. Of the 41,309 sorties flown during *Operation Desert Storm,* only 20 per cent were against strategic targets, primarily due to low availability of PGMs and absence of real-time target information, a figure that went up significantly in 2003, as the coalition forces increased the number of PGMs used to almost 65 per cent of the total bombs dropped. Another interesting change in the US strategy in 2003, which has lessons for the Indian Air Force, is that the strategic air campaign during the 2003 Iraq war was not tied to any traditional timetable[30] and was made to fit like a glove around simultaneous

---

29 'Ten Propositions regarding Air Power', Col. Philip Meilinger, *Air Power Journal,* Spring 1996, pp. 51–59.

land and naval campaigns that gave more impetus to the importance of synergy and joint operations.

Asset Allocation

The present force structure of the IAF offers limited capability for 'Strategic Intervention'. Only aircraft like the SU-30 MKI and IL-76/78 meet the various criteria laid down for strategic intervention. Given India's growing global aspirations, there is a need to address our force structure requirements for strategic force projection, intervention and even coercive diplomacy. While delivering the Air Chief Marshal PC Lal memorial lecture in March 2006, the then Honourable Raksha Mantri of India, Shri Pranab Mukherjee acknowledged the primacy of air power in future conflicts and linked the re-orientation of the IAF to India's rapid economic growth and the need to protect our security interests, extending from the Persian Gulf to the Malacca Straits. He went on to also highlight[31] the need for emphasis on strategic thinking, joint operations and asymmetric warfare, all of which have been discussed in this article. Some of the essential ingredients to bolster our strategic air war fighting capability are listed below. These include not only tangible assets, like hardware resources and technology, but also intangibles, like leadership and political will. The list includes:

- Platforms
- Facilitators
- Information providers
- Responsible and knowledge-based leadership
- Political will and speedy decision-making organisation.
- **Platforms** Amongst the numerous aerial platforms that are presently in use the world over as part of 'Strategic Forces', the most important ones from an Indian perspective are fighter ac, heavy-lift/medium-lift transport ac, multi-role helicopters, and force multipliers like AWACS, AAR platforms and EW aircraft. These platforms need to be backed up by real-time information providers, like Satellites with < 1 m resolution and rapidly deployable UAVs with multiple sensors, adequate loiter time and even limited fire power. While the SU-30 MKI with its phenomenal reach, awesome fire power, multicrew and multi msn capability is an ideal platform to prosecute a strategic air campaign, it is important that we clearly understand that essentially tactical platforms like the

30   Ibid.
31   Honourable Raksha Mantri of India, Shri Pranab Mukherjee, Speaking at the Air Marshal P C Lal memorial lecture on 20 March 2006, *Defence Watch*, April 2006, pp. 8–10.

M-2000 and the MMRCA (Medium Multi-Role Combat Aircraft), 126 of which are in the pipeline, can be employed effectively in neutralising 'strategic targets'. Even older platforms like the Jaguar can supplement the SU-30s M-2000s and the MRCA, the only caveat being that greater coordination, support and precision would be required for using them in the strategic air campaign. Strategic strike capability without strategic airlift capability leaves a gaping hole in a nation's ability to project, sustain, reinforce and if required, even extricate strategic forces over large distances. The IAF's only strategic airlift platform, the IL-76, is ageing and needs to be supplemented by a newer generation heavy-lift aircraft in the same or larger category and a medium-lift aircraft in the 15-20 tonne payload category. As far as helicopters are concerned, destruction of C3I nodes, elimination of leadership, insertion/exfiltration of Special Forces and interdiction of reserves and follow-on forces are all strategic tasks if one looks at effect-based operations. A yawning deficiency in this area exists and needs to be addressed at the earliest.

- **Force Multipliers** With the induction of the IL-78 AAR platform and the impending induction of AWACS, the IAF would have taken the first step in becoming a truly self-reliant air force with global intervention capability. However, let us not be lulled into a false sense of bravado that the journey ends here. If one looks at the geographical extent of our country one would realize that the number of refuellers and AWACS would barely suffice to address tactical needs in multiple theatres leaving very little for any meaningful strategic intervention. It is this limitation and void that needs to be filled with additional inductions to create an exclusive force that thinks, trains and fights 'strategically', more of which will be discussed in organisational and training imperatives later on in the article. The induction of UAVs and exploitation of civilian space technology has also added significant punch to our capability, and needs to be well integrated into our intelligence framework.

Intelligence Gathering to Support Strategic Air Ops

Presently, sharing of intelligence between the military and other agencies leaves much to be desired and turf battles have resulted in 'below optimal', sharing of both hard and soft intelligence. Targets for strategic intervention are no longer static and range from elusive enemy leadership to highly mobile tactical weapon systems, whose destruction can break an enemy's will to continue fighting. Classic examples of this were the continued Air US attacks against mobile Al Quaida leadership with limited success in conjunction with Special Forces and the destruction of Serb SAGW sites during the Kosovo conflict by air power alone.

There are presently too many agencies that receive, process, interpret and disseminate intelligence, and there is a pressing need for a lean intelligence structure to support strategic air operations. Without dissecting the structure too critically, a broad requirement is given below in Figure 1.1:

Figure 1.1

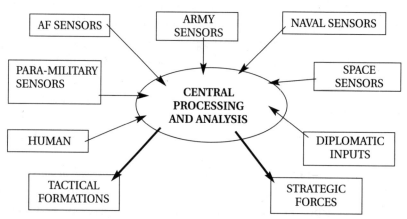

With the phasing out of the MiG-25 strategic reconnaissance aircraft, the onus of providing accurate intelligence for strategic targeting has shifted to space-based sensors. Even in the absence of dedicated military satellites, capabilities of civilian remote-sensing technologies like the Ikonos (USA) and the Indian TES permit resolutions as low as 1m[32]. With possibilities of further reduction in resolution on the anvil, the dividing gap between civilian and military capability is reducing. Typical resolution of some possible strategic targets in metres is given in Table 1.2[33]:

---

32   U R Rao, 'National Reconnaissance Assets Required for Military Intelligence', *Trishul*, Spring 2003, pp 50–54.

33   Ibid.

Table 1.2 Resolution for Targeting

Target	Detection	General Identification	Precise Identification	Description	Techn- ical Analysis
C3I HQs	3	1.5	1.0	.15	.10
Nuclear Wpn Compone nts	2.5	1.5	1.0	.15	.05
Missile Sites	3	1	1.0	.3	.05
Airfd Facilities	6	4	3	.3	.15
Bridge	6	4	1.5	1.0	.3
Radar	3	1	.3	.15	.02
Supply Dump	2	1	0.3	.03	.03

According to Prof UR Rao, one of the pioneers of India's satellite programme, the only way to exploit space for strategic intelligence is to foster greater synergy between ISRO and defence users, like the three services, RAW and the IB.[34] He further goes on to say that all requirements for strategic reconnaissance have to be met indigenously, with ISRO being capable of meeting reduced resolution requirements. Needless to say, the success of any strategic air campaign depends on the accuracy of intelligence and training in a realistic environment like the coalition forces carried out in *Operation Desert Shield* prior to *Operation Desert Storm*. Common sensor and communications programmes in UAVs, manned ac and even satellites are vital for mission effectiveness along with a single processing, analysing and disseminating agency like the Aerial Common Sensor programme being adopted by the US armed forces.[35]

Communication Requirements

Transfer of real-time information between platforms and ground/air-borne sensors is vital for the successful execution of any mission and assumes even greater relevance in the case of a Strategic Air Operation wherein the flexibility to abort the operation or a new target location could be given minutes before the TOT (Time Over Target), something that is imperative to ensure success of the

34   Ibid.
35   Robert Wall & David Fulgheu, Sigint Snarl Aviation Week & Space Technology, January 23, 2006, p. 24.

emerging concept of 'just in time' targeting. Some of the ingredients of a secure, effective and flexible system are highlighted below:

- A satellite-based defence communication system with encryption and sufficient bandwidth
- Link 16 type of data-linking facilities that give aircrew and mission coordinators a clear picture or situation report of both the tactical and strategic air situation. This would involve elaborate linking up of surveillance platforms, ground-processing sensors, AWACS, airborne platforms and even Special Forces who could be assigned the role of terminal designators against mobile and elusive targets, like enemy leadership in mountainous terrain.

Political Will and Intent

Prosecution of the strategic air campaign requires strong political will, clarity of intent and the ability to gather domestic public support/approval and absorb international flak and criticism. The only way to gather public support in a democracy like India is to encourage widespread strategic debates so that our strategic interests are widely known and accepted, and when these interests are threatened, the decision to use force can easily be taken. This is a weak area in our country and needs to be addressed at the earliest. The organisation for speedy decision making exists. It only needs to be exercised in the direction of strategic interests and intervention more often.

Changes in Philosophy/Doctrine

Probably the most difficult part of change is to alter a mindset. The past 30 years have shown that air power has the ability to decisively influence the course of any conflict by strategic application of aerial force, be it in the Arab Israeli conflicts of 1967, in Bekaa Valley in 1982, or during the conflicts in Iraq, Afghanistan and Kosovo. It is time to embrace a doctrinal shift towards building up a strategic forces command that recognizes the need to develop intervention capability spearheaded by air power with naval and land forces completing a synergistic troika without needlessly engaging in turf battles regarding command and control of theatre forces, something that has so often stunted the development of strategic doctrine within the Indian armed forces. There is a need to adopt techniques of parallel warfare in which the payoffs of strategic application of airpower, when applied simultaneously with tactical application, acts as a decisive force. Lest the surface forces feel that the impact of strategic air strikes is not felt at the tactical or operational levels of war, one does not have to go very far back in history. The use of tactical platforms like A-10s, AV-8Bs, and F/A-18s to destroy elements of the two Iraqi Armoured Divisions that were seen to manoeuvre offensively to influence the abortive Iraqi offensive at Al-Khafji is a classic example of a tactical operation that ultimately had tremendous strategic significance in that it proved to be the proverbial 'nail in the coffin' for Iraqi ground resistance in1991.[36] Contrary to early theorists like Douhet and Mitchell, who believed that Strategic Air Attacks alone can win a war, the concept of the strategic air campaign today focuses on attacking targets that can subsequently be attacked or exploited by surface forces with reduced forces and reduced casualties. Current air force doctrines seek to serve the overall effort by leveraging the impact of strategic strikes and interdiction and not wage independent wars.[37] This in itself should be enough to assuage any apprehension amongst the surface forces that air power is trying to usurp the primacy of surface forces. Such a belief is a total non-issue and only undermines synergy and jointmanship. The key issue, however, is to foster an understanding of the capabilities of Strategic strikes and interdiction. Despite the politico-strategic procrastination of using airpower during the Kargil conflict,[38] the IAF's 'never done before' high altitude interdiction air campaign did contribute significantly to the strategic objective of evicting Pakistani regulars and Mujahedin from the heights that they had stealthily and audaciously occupied. With that as a template, there is nothing that prevents the formulation of a cohesive interdiction campaign, provided the surface forces realise the tremendous pay-offs of a well-planned strategic interdiction campaign.

Training

The next logical step after displaying the political will and changing existing mindsets regarding the advantages of air power in the furtherance of India's strategic objectives is to train and think to fight strategically. The present training pattern in the IAF for aircrew, controllers and support elements is heavily skewed towards tactical orientation and is rather defensive in nature, given our reactive doctrine, for we have never wanted to be seen as an aggressive and expansionist country. Without drastically altering our training methodology, there is a need to train continuously in strategic roles. A strategic orientation can be introduced at the training stage itself after induction of the

---

36   Lt. Col. Price T. Bingham (Retd.), USAF Revolutionizing Warfare Throuh Interdiction, *Air Power Journal*, Spring 96.
37   Ibid, n.4, Mark J.Conversino.
38   Gen. V. P. Malik, *Kargil: From Surprise to Victory*, Harper Collins.

Hawk AJT, in which trainee pilots could be introduced to Air-to-Air-Refuelling (AAR) and long-distance missions in the final phase of training.

Some areas that need immediate attention are enumerated below:

- Simulated target systems need to be created on the lines that exist in the Negev desert of Israel, which cater to wide-ranging scenarios, from evacuation of personnel to destruction of key installations and terrorist eliminations. These targets need to be engaged across the country in different seasons and terrain.
- A pool of specially trained aircrew on varied platforms needs to be formed, which is primarily tactically proficient but also undergoes periodic specialist capsules and training in execution of strategic missions. This core group on different fleets needs to be exercised periodically.
- Regular yearly/half-yearly exercises involving joint task forces at varied locations ranging from deserts to hilly terrain and island territories need to be conducted. Long-distance missions involving AAR, change in control zones, height bands and time zones may be regularly planned. Sleep deprivation and fatigue orientation[39] needs to be introduced at regular intervals.
- Multiple aerial refuellings and engagements spread across theatres must be introduced at various levels of squadron training.
- Strategic airlift capability and helicopter operations along with special forces must be given impetus and exercised periodically.
- Exercises with a few foreign air forces must be continued with simulation of contingencies in mutually acceptable third countries.
- Strategic task forces need to be created with centralized decision-making, independent component commanders, and decentralised execution.

India-Centric Summary

With the phasing out of a number of squadrons of MiG-21s, 23s, and 27s, the IAF's fighter fleet is in a period of transition.[40] The transport and helicopter fleets in the IAF are also due for expansion and refurbishment, with emphasis on replacements for the AN-32 and IL-76 and the induction of a medium-lift ac in the 15–20 tonne category. No replacement has been identified for the Mi-8/Cheetah/Chetak, although the ALH is waiting on the wings. The

39   Ibid,n.1.
40   Ibid,n. 9.

modernisation process is likely to take 10–15 years, by the end of which the IAF will possess significant strategic capability in terms of platforms and force multipliers. These would not be an area of concern. The main areas of concern are related to infrastructural requirements to support such operations, communications, political will to prosecute strategic air operations and sister service support and acknowledgement of the long-term strategic payoffs of such operation. The IAF's mindset also has to shift from being a tactically oriented and proficient force to one that has the confidence to influence strategy and doctrinal changes. At a time when nations are increasingly reluctant to commit ground forces due to the 'body bag' effect, the ability to engage strategic targets with minimum collateral damage and maximum effect has made air power a 'most preferred option' in swift conflict resolution. The main problems that have to be dealt with while prosecuting the strategic air campaign mainly would relate to morality, legality[41] and accuracy of intelligence. From the horrific aerial attacks on London, Coventry, Dresden and Berlin to the precision with which targets were engaged in Afghanistan and Iraq in 2003, the strategic air campaign has come a long way and it is about time that the IAF puts together a blueprint for building a credible strategic aerial intervention capability over the next decade.

Eleven Cardinal Principles of the Strategic Air Campaign

- Aerospace power of any kind, which directly influences or achieves the strategic objectives of a campaign, would be classified as part of the Strategic Air Campaign (SAC).
- Political will is the key to the effective implementation of the SAC.
- Centralized command of all forces involved in the SAC, coupled with decentralized execution and minimum political interference, is a vital imperative for the success of the SAC.
- Target selection remains a predominantly politico-military process, while target engagement is a purely military one.
- Flexibility, surprise and shock effect are the key ingredients of a successful and contemporary SAC.
- 'Effect-based operations' and not platform based is the cornerstone of such operations.
- The SAC cannot be an isolated and time-based campaign. It has to be intelligently dovetailed into the surface campaign, and best precedes it by surprising the enemy and blunting his will to fight.

---

41   Thomas Keany, 'Air Power : What a Difference a Decade Makes', Foreign Policy Institute, John Hopkins University, February 9, 2005.

- The SAC is best employed as part of the emerging concept of 'parallel warfare', in which all forms of combat power are unleashed simultaneously.
- Accurate and 'real-time intelligence' allows the SAC to transcend conventional barriers and adopt 'just in time targeting' techniques, which until very recently was exclusively a tactical option.
- Use of PGMs ensures achievement of objectives with minimum effort, attrition and collateral damage.
- Creation of a credible and potent strategic force to prosecute the SAC can only come about if there are changes in mindsets at all levels that we have entered a new era of warfare[42] and that of airpower being essentially a 'tactical tool'. Doctrinal changes will be slow, difficult and fraught with obstacles.

---

42   Thomas A. Keany and Eliot Cohen, Air Power Survey-Summary Report, Washington D.C, 1993.

CRYSTAL GAZING INTO THE FUTURE THE IAF FIGHTER FLEET IN 2025

Aviators who look too much into the future are considered a trifle whimsical; in fact, they are considered to be mavericks. Unfortunately, when what they predict comes true, all they can do is chuckle from their graves.

-Billy Mitchell

This paper assumes significance at a time when the Government of India has floated a Request for Proposal for the purchase of 126 MMRCA aircraft for the IAF.

In order to cope with the rapidly changing geopolitical environment and constantly changing threat perceptions, there is a need to crystal gaze into the future and envisage what kind of force structure would be required 20 years from now. In order to do so, a number of questions needs to be answered. Some of the prominent ones are: What are the significant geopolitical changes envisaged in 2025? What is India's pecking in the world order likely to be? Are there going to be any significant changes in the military threat scenarios? These and many more need to be answered before embarking on a force structure study for the future. By 2025, the only fighter ac in the IAF's present inventory that would still be in service is the SU-30 MKI. These would barely make up 10 squadrons against an existing force structure of 45 squadrons, which could at best be pared to 35+ squadrons due to overriding economic constraints. It is, therefore, extremely vital to systematically approach the problem of restructuring the fighter fleet over the next 20 years, keeping in mind the importance of encouraging indigenous development without compromising on quality and adherence to the various ASRs laid down by the IAF. Equally important is the need to factor in various geopolitical, economic and RMA imperatives. Only such an approach will ensure that the cutting edge of the IAF remains a potent and effective instrument of our military potential despite a possible reduction in force levels.

A good starting point would be to skim through a few critical macro-geopolitical developments, economic and military imperatives and likely conflict situations before deciding on certain critical paradigms for force structure planning. Any force structure changes in the future, would obviously be accompanied by significant enhancement in force multiplier capability and infrastructural support, two areas that are critical to the effectiveness of a lean but technology-intensive force like the fighter fleet. Also discussed later in the article would be the likely problem areas in our quest for the right balance in terms of fleet/role mix and timely replacements for ageing aircraft.

Current Geopolitical Imperatives

The period 1990–2005 saw a few critical macro-geopolitical developments that dictated force structure requirements. The most obvious and important development has to be the collapse of the Soviet Union and the emergence of a unipolar world with the US as the sole superpower. The break-up of the Soviet Union did create a problem for the IAF in terms of a slowdown in flow of spares and maintainability of the MiG fleets that comprise more than 70 per cent of the total fighter fleet. The rapid spread of Islamic Fundamentalism and its associated terror networks have opened up new battlefields and challenges for the IAF that would probably necessitate a change in philosophy in terms of a clear articulation of intent in a LICO scenario when it comes to effective employment of fighter assets. The emergence of *regional hotspots based on ethno-religious aspirations* like in the Balkans, Chechnya and Afghanistan was the next important happening along with increased UN/multilateral intervention in peace-keeping and peace enforcement operations in the Balkans, various countries in the troubled, African continent, Afghanistan and Iraq. As far as India specifically is concerned, the IAF's force structure remained Pakistan-centric with emphasis on conventional war fighting capability with limited nuclear delivery capability. While the long-term primary threat remained China, economic compulsions prevented India from reorganising its force structure to exclusively cater to a Chinese threat. Instead, it engaged China in a productive, de-escalation dialogue that allowed both countries to shift focus on economic progress. Whether this détente, which is highly desirable, will continue till 2025 is both debatable and doubtful.

Geopolitical Imperatives 2005–2025

India Surrounded by Failed States
The likelihood of India being surrounded by failed states over the next decade or two cannot be ruled out. Sri Lanka is likely to continue in ferment as long as

the LTTE is active. Support for the separatist elements is likely to continue from Tamil Nadu. Pakistan is unlikely to stabilize and chances of its plunging into 'Islamic anarchy' cannot be ruled out. Pakistan, in its present or its predicted chaotic state may continue to support terrorism and wage sporadic 'Proxy Wars'. Nepal is likely to continue to see a power struggle amongst the monarchy, the Maoists and pro-democracy elements. Further to the east, the stability of the 'Soft Eastern Flank' of our country, which is vulnerable because of porous borders and disparate ethnic groups that will continue to trouble India. Infiltration of Islamic fundamentalism from Bangladesh is a live threat that has ominous warnings to the stability of our country. Porous borders with Nepal and Bangladesh may become breeding areas for terrorists/insurgent camps. What implications would such a scenario have on our fighter fleet composition? Any effective intervention or show of force in LICO/CI scenarios in these areas cannot be restricted to the employment of only attack/armed helicopters. There is a need to look at a small but effective complement of fighter aircraft that can deploy as part of a Rapid Reaction Force. In the immediate future, the Hawk can perform this role, but for the future, due thought needs to be given to this role.

The China Factor

China is always known to progress 'cyclically'. Its present cycle of economic progress is only half done and may take another 10–15 years to bear the desired result. Once that cycle is complete, it is almost certain that China would increasingly flex its muscles militarily. There can be no doubt that China sees India as a rival for both economic and military dominance of the region. However, it also sees the futility of engaging in any form of direct conflict with India and would prefer to engage in 'deterrence' of various kinds and at the same time continue to exert both covert and overt influence in India's neighbourhood with prime focus on the Indian Ocean region, Myanmar, Bangladesh and Nepal. However, any threat vis-à-vis China has to look at both the land-dominated Northern/Eastern theatre and the maritime theatre in the Bay of Bengal extending up to the Malacca Straits. China may exert pressure on Andaman & Nicobar via its increased influence in Myanmar and the Coco islands. Its navy is bound to step up forays into the Indian Ocean and the Malacca Straits. With the acquisition of SU-30s, the PLAAF may increasingly use Tibetan airspace for training and 'muscle flexing'. To cater for the entire Chinese front in the north and eastern sectors, a major portion, if not the entire fighter fleet has to be capable of high-altitude operations and weapon delivery, coupled with adequate range. On the maritime front, a capability must be built up to exert influence from the air up to areas around the Malacca Straits and even the South China Sea. Needless to say, this influence can be exerted only with sustainable force multiplier effort in the form of Flight Refuelling Aircraft and AWACS.

US Influence

In its continuing endeavour to maintain a unipolar world, the US has been increasingly looking eastwards. India meets all the criteria that the US is looking for in a 'Strategic Partner' in the Asia Pacific region to counter China, Russia and Islamic fundamentalism. Whether India will 'bite the bullet' as far as the NSSP (Next Step in Strategic Partnership) as outlined by President Bush, is too early to predict as long as the 'Left' plays an important role in our coalition politics. It would suffice to say that it would be one of the most critical decisions that India has to make in the 21st century. How it influences our 'Force Structure' planning would be discussed later in the paper.

Economic Imperatives

Budgetary allocation for defence expenditure in terms of percentage of GDP is likely to see a visible decline. However, in real terms, the allocation would rise significantly, considering India's expected sustained growth rate of 6–10 per cent over the next 15–20 years. Innovative and imaginative budget management would be required to get more 'bang for the buck'. Juggling of capital and revenue expenditure, earmarking of funds for outright purchases vis-à-vis phased payments and funds for indigenous development of ac and systems for the LCA and any future fighter development are amongst the areas of concern that need to be addressed. In all probability, budgetary constraints could force the IAF to reduce the number of squadrons from 40 to an acceptably lower figure.

Critical Paradigms for Force Structure Planning

There are certain critical paradigms on which any fresh thinking on force structure planning needs to be based. These paradigms would be based on the various geopolitical, environmental and technological changes that would influence operations of the force that you wish to restructure. In this case they would directly or indirectly impinge on the fighter fleet of the IAF. Some of the critical ones are:

- Transformation from a 'number intensive fleet' to a 'capability intensive fleet'
- Rapid reaction capability
- Exercising the 'Depth Option'. This basically implies that fighter aircraft should be able to operate from moderate states of readiness and from bases in depth.
- Expanding India's sphere of influence. Indian forces may have to intervene in potential hotspots like Afghanistan, Iran, Central Asian Republics and even Indonesia and Taiwan as part of an International Force.
- Increased reliance on indigenous space-based intelligence gathering systems apart from UCAV/UAV-based SIGINT, SEAD, ELINT and Recce. Increased sharing of targeting functions by SSMs
- Increased dependence on force multipliers and their complete integration
- Need for quantum improvement in infrastructure and communications to support inter and intra-theatre operations.

Current Force Structure

A broad and realistic overview of the present force structure along with fleet-wise employability would be in order so as to identify gaps that would need to be plugged when planning for the future. The MiG-21 FL or T-77 fleet that perform the role of LIFT (Lead-in-Fighter Training) is likely to be phased out in the next few years and replaced by the HAWK AJT. The MiG-21 M fleet that performs various Ground Attack, Recce and training roles would also be phased out, probably around 2010 and so would the remaining MiG-23 squadrons. The RFP (Request for Proposal) for 120+ MRCA ac that has been floated by the IAF is primarily to plug this gap. Even though the MiG-27 and Jaguar fleets are in the midst of an upgrade programme, these aircraft are, most optimistically, unlikely to last beyond 2020. The MiG-29 and MiG-21 Bison fleets, which presently complement the SU-30 and Mirage-2000 in Air Defence roles are also likely to be phased out by 2015 and 2020 respectively. Last of all, we look at the Mirage-2000 and SU-30 fleets, the punch of the IAF with multi-role capability. The present lot of Mirage-2000s would be reaching the end of their useful employability by 2020 and the present lot of Su-30s would have completed their mid-life upgrades and looking for sustenance. Therefore, to reiterate, only the SU-30 fleet would remain in 2025, clearly indicating that the next 20 years would have to see inductions of a magnitude that the IAF has never seen before

The two major decisions that would need to be taken during the process of fleet modernization and replacement relate to fleet mix and role mix. The present fleet mix is in the ratio of almost 1:4 in favour of ac of Russian Origin. The dependence of Russian origin on ac has not reduced since the collapse of the Soviet Union and though the SU-30 MKI is a good mix of Russian design and Western systems there is a need to consciously address the issue of over-dependence on one block. With the US and France pitching in strongly with the F-16/F-18/Rafale following the RFI (Request for Intent) by the IAF for 120 + fighter ac, this imbalance is likely to addressed even through the MiG-35 is also a contender. Indigenisation would remain a thrust area and the IAF needs to support the LCA project, if not for its quality and role effectiveness but as a hedge against foreign dominance.

Presently the IAF has ac with specific and multi-role capability. The Jaguar and MiG-29 being examples of dedicated GA and AD ac while the SU-30 MKI and M-2000 are ac with Multi Role capability. The financial viability of role specific ac has been much debated, with the balance the world over having shifted to multi-role and swing role capability. The IAF may well have to follow suit and this would have to be factored in prior to deciding on futuristic fleet composition.

Scenarios for Force Structure Planning

Are there going to be any significant changes in the roles that the IAF would be called upon to perform in likely conflict scenarios in 2025? Even at the cost of repetition, some that immediately come to mind are rapid reaction capability as a complement of a rapid reaction force, enhanced joint operations, especially in sub-conventional scenarios, participation in multinational/multilateral peace keeping/peace enforcement operations, enforcement of 'No Fly' zones, protection of island territories, maritime interest and extended spheres of influence if any, and sustained operations at high altitude areas.

Proposed Force Structure

Based on the economic viability of maintaining a technology intensive force that is reinforced with adequate force multipliers and infrastructure capability, a slight reduction in terms of sheer numbers cannot be ruled out. How then would the force look like in 2025? It must also be remembered that for a country of India's size, technology cannot be seen as an alternative to numbers considering the number of commitments in terms of areas of interest and likely conflict.

Proposed Force Structure (Fighter Fleet) — 2025

Sl. No.	Type of ac	Strength	Role	Remarks
1	SU-30 MKI	8–10 Squadrons	Multi-role capability	Specialist roles to be assigned to all Squadrons.
2	MMRCA (F-16/18/M-200-5/Gripen/MiG-35)	7–8 Squadrons	Multi-role capability	Licensed manufacture is the key to the deal.
3	LCA **	04 Squadrons	AD/CSFO	Unlikely to last till 2025.
4	Hawk **	4 Squadrons	Training /CSFO	May not last till 2025.
5	Dedicated fixed wing ac for anti-insurgency ops	4 Squadrons	Counter-insurgency capability located alongside each army command. As part of JTFs.	RFI may have to be floated soon. IAF may have to look at combining the AJT and counter-insurgency capability.
6	Multi-role next generation ac with global reach of the F-22/JSF class	8–10 Squadrons	Multi-role capability	RFI would have to floated soon.

** Likely to be phased out by 2025 with typical prospects of life extensions in case no replacements are finalized.

The following resource constraints have been factored in to arrive at the structure. The present 40 Squadron force levels have been trimmed to a leaner and more sophisticated force with true multi-role capability. As can be seen, the entire force structure would revolve around three main multi-role platforms, viz. Su-30 MKI, MMRCA and F-22/JSF class of futuristic fighters. The reduced fixed wing force levels have been arrived at after considering the possibilities of increased induction of UCAVs, UAVs and SSMs. The following considerations in fleet composition merit attention.

- **SU-30 MKI Fleet** The fleet would have to assume true multi-role capability with each squadron being assigned a 'core' or 'super specialized role'. The sustainability of this fleet past 2025 is vital for our security needs with progressive updates being periodically planned.
- **M-2000/MMRCA Fleet** Role assignment for the ac that are slated to replace the MiG-21s need to be very clearly thought-out during the contractual phase itself so that systems integration and upgrades are planned accordingly. These ac must be optimized for high altitude operations and capable of delivering a variety of PGMs and conventional munitions. The experience gained during *Op Safed Sagar* must be factored in while selecting this class of ac.
- **LCA** Induction of LCA is very critical for filling in gaps that exist in our AD network when it comes to having adequate number of interceptors for Limited Area AD, a role presently being undertaken by MiG-21s. Additionally, the LCA needs to be optimised for the CSFO role to replace the MiG-27 and T-96 and supplement the Hawks. Increased IAF involvement in the LCA project is the only cost-effective way forward. All attempts must be made to sustain at least part of the LCA fleet beyond 2025. These ac could be assigned the CSFO/counter insurgency roles.
- **Dedicated Anti-Counter Insurgency AC** To enhance jointmanship and provide fighter support in addition to helicopter support to counter-insurgency operations, there may be a need to acquire an ac dedicated to this role that can also be used for close support ops. The Hawk may assume this war-time role, if modified suitably. However, a dedicated ac may have to be thought of, considering the nature of conflict that is envisaged twenty years from now.
- **Induction of Fifth Generation fighter Aircraft** If India does progress the NSSP (Next Step in Strategic Partnership) with the US, the IAF should seriously consider bolstering our intra theatre and global reach capability with a limited acquisition of the F-22 and JSF class of ac after they have entered active service with the USAF and proved themselves. Alternatively, there would be a need to design and develop and indigenous ac of the above class and build on the expertise gathered in the LCA project incorporating additional features, like stealth technology.

Conceptual Changes

Three of the important conceptual changes that may influence the force structure of 2025 are discussed below. These are:

- **Depth Option** The 'depth' option would imply that strategic and high-value fighter assets and Force Multipliers like FRA and AWACS ac would only be located at bases in depth with forward bases only performing early warning and turnaround functions with limited assets. This would imply that EW and Intelligence gathering assets like Aerostats, UCAVs, UAVs and LL EW radars would be located at forward area airfields with periodic activation by AD ac. This would necessitate massive infrastructure requirement at bases in the 'hinterland' that provide adequate strategic depth.

- **Force Multiplier Requirements** As a corollary of the depth option, there would be the need to have at least three Squadrons of Flight Refuelling Aircraft and two squadrons of AWACS comprising at least 8–10 ac. This would take care of operations in at least two theatres simultaneously with adequate reserve or various combinations of overseas deployments. With this, surveillance in the large Western and Eastern theatres would be catered for, along with some attention to our vast maritime interest zones in conjunction with other naval surveillance assets. Additionally, as mentioned earlier, UAVs, UCAVs and SSMs would take on a number of roles that are presently performed by our fighter fleet.
- **Extent of Engagement with the US** If India steps up its engagement with the US and emerges as a key strategic ally with a comprehensive asset-sharing arrangement, a number of areas in fighter force re-structuring may benefit directly or indirectly from this alliance. For instance, the LCA project could get a mid-life boost in terms of an upgrade programme, fighter acquisitions of aircraft like the F-22 and JSF with licensed manufacturing may be a preferred option, sharing of force multipliers and intelligence may ease pressure on budgetary constraints and leasing of bases could give a fillip to infrastructural development.

Infrastructure Support

Infrastructure support for the envisaged force structure has to be in place to ensure sustainability and optimal utilisation of the various fleets. This would include:

- Better maintained Operating Surfaces and creation of dispersal facilities, like underground shelters and blast pens that are insulated from the effects of NBC warfare.
- Upgradation of Armament Storage and arming facilities to cater for new generation PGMs and missiles along with mechanised weapon-handling capability.
- Seamless and secure connectivity with secure and instant communications, primarily to support a vast integrated AD network.

- Data links for both air defence and ground attack roles. This would also entail induction of airborne, satellite-aided targeting platforms and target-sharing devices like J STARS.

Problem Areas

While it is very easy to crystal gaze into the future and draw up fancy wish-lists, it is equally important to do a reality check and visualize the problems areas as we go along. A chronological visualization of the problem areas relating to the IAF's fighter acquisition programme would go a long way in finding solutions and drawing up contingency plans. Some of these are:

- **Replacement of MiG-21s** The first challenge faced by the IAF would be to find suitable replacements for all the variants of the MiG-21, MiG-23 and MiG-27s in reasonable time frames. This exercise has already commenced, albeit rather late, and is likely to face many hurdles, primarily on the political front. Contingency plans should primarily look at operating with reduced force levels and not at life extension of old fleets.
- **Induction of LCA** Delayed induction of LCA is almost a certainty. This should not deter the IAF from supporting the programme as it is a huge step in self reliance. Due caution must be exercised to ensure that HAL focuses on internal deliveries to the IAF and meeting the various Air Staff Requirements of the IAF rather than export ambitions. Increased IAF involvement in the development of a next generation fighter is another key issue that would have to be addressed sooner than later.
- **Jaguar, MiG-29 and Bison Replacement** Chronologically, the next dilemma faced by the IAF would be to select a replacement for the Jaguar and MiG-29. This too is likely to be a contentious issue, probably with an intense debate on whether a multi-role platform can do what the Jaguar and MiG-29 do. A similar exercise would have to commence for a replacement for the MiG-21 Bison. A JSF class of ac would ideally fill the void created by the phasing out of the Jaguars, MiG-29 and the Bison.
- **SU-30 MKI and MRCA** Unless the mid-life upgrades on the SU-30 MKI and the 100 + ac that are likely to be bought soon are planned between 2015 and 2020, finding a suitable replacement for the SU-30 MKI post-2025 is going to be an extremely daunting proposition.
- **Upgrades on FRA/AWACs** Just as the KC-135 and the E-3 Sentry have undergone a number of upgrades over the last 25 years, a similar programme must be initiated on the IL-78 and our AWACS platform.

- **Replacement for Hawks** By 2025 the Hawk AJT would have to be replaced by a suitable AJT with suitable CSFO/counter-insurgency capability.

Recommendations

To summarise what has been articulated in the article and to sustain a reasonably modern 35+ squadron fighter fleet in 2025, the following measures need to be implemented over a period of time.

- Finalisation of replacement ac for T-77s, T-96, MiG-23 MF and MiG-23 BN with the MMRCA must be completed by 2007, so that deliveries commence from 2009.
- Induction of LCA must be ensured by 2008, with at least one squadron being inducted every year.
- Replacements for the Jaguar, old M-2000 Squadrons, MiG-29 Squadrons and MiG-21 Bisons with approximately 10–12 squadrons of F-22 and JSF class of ac must be finalised by 2015 to ensure smooth transition. Alternatively, indigenous development of a futuristic fighter needs to be accelerated, for which specific ASRs need to be formulated by the IAF.
- Adequate emphasis be placed on availability of force multipliers like FRA and AWACS to ensure maximum exploitation of fighter fleet capability. A total of three FRA squadrons with 8–10 ac each and at least two squadrons of AWACs with 8-10 ac would be the bare minimum to exploit the multi-role capability of all ac.
- Infrastructure, networking and communication requirements need to be addressed on priority for ensuring optimum utilisation and preservation of assets.

Long-range and perspective planning in the IAF has always been hampered by delayed political decision making and lack of synergy at times between the IAF and HAL. This has resulted in a crunch situation for the IAF wherein a number of MiG variants are due to be phased out without suitable replacements. While this is of immediate priority, unless we anticipate the requirements of 2025, there is a distinct possibility that the IAF repeats today's mistakes tomorrow. It is precisely for this reason that this exercise needs to be undertaken with synergy and foresight. Only then can we expect to have a potent fighter fleet that has the capability of serving as a powerful instrument of India's global and regional ambitions with its reach, flexibility and fire power.

OUT-OF-COUNTRY CONTINGENCY OPERATIONS

The experience at Kandahar exposed the inability of the state to effectively protect our interests outside our geographical boundaries and served as a wake-up call for us to develop capabilities to do so. This article is an attempt to showcase the potential of air power to act as a credible instrument of national power **This paper was presented at The Subroto Memorial Seminar at the India Habitat Centre on 31 December 2006.**

If we do decide to commit forces to combat overseas, we should have clearly defined political and military objectives. And we should precisely how know our forces can achieve those objectives.

Abstract

India's expanding footprints of influence and her emerging aspirations of becoming a truly competitive global power has made it imperative for her to look at developing capabilities that can control, mitigate or diffuse beyond her geographical boundaries, events that have a direct or indirect bearing on her strategic interests. Military capability alone cannot perform this role. It has to be effectively supplemented by a strong political will, diplomatic initiatives, synergistic sharing of intelligence and sensitised media and public support. Military capability in turn has to comprise all those assets that would ensure presence, coercive capability, fire power, sustainability, and the capabilities to speed up rehabilitation and relief. It is in the light of these imperatives that we need to take a closer look at the role of air power in Out-of-Country Contingencies (OCC), without diluting the essence of such operations, viz. Interoperability in a Combined Arms approach, involving the entire range of land, maritime and air operations.

Background

The last few years have seen the Indian strategic community venture into hitherto uncharted territory, and attempt to discuss contingency planning, should Indian interests be threatened across the globe. These discussions have been sporadic, hampered frequently by poor tri-service inter-operability and most important, lacking clear-cut politico-military direction in the form of clear government policy directives. Even the recently published *Joint Doctrine of the Indian Armed Forces* makes only a superficial mention of Out-of-Area Operations and stays clear of articulating any definitive intervention philosophy and force structure composition.

Some of the main reasons for our reluctance to discuss OCC could have been:

- Delayed realisation of our global potential and the concurrent desire to be perceived as a leader of the developing world against hegemony by the 'super powers'
- Excessive faith in the UN and reluctance to commit forces to multilateral forces/coalition forces

- Preoccupation with internal security problems and an unwillingness/lack of capability to strike at the root of these threats, even if known to be on foreign soil
- Lack of technology and fire power to conduct swift and surgical missions similar to the ones carried out by Israel at Entebbe, the Osirak strike and *Op El Dorado Canyon* over Libya.

In the wake of the Cold War, attention has been focused on a rising number of territorial disputes, armed ethnic conflicts, and civil wars that pose threats to regional and international peace and may be accompanied by natural or manmade disasters which precipitate massive human suffering. We have learned that effective responses to these situations may require multi-dimensional operations composed of such components as political/diplomatic, humanitarian, intelligence, economic development, and synergised military operations. It is only recently that India's region of Strategic Interest was defined in the Ministry of Defence's (MoD) Annual Report 2002–2003 as extending from the Central Asian Republics in the north to the area encompassing the Indian Ocean region (IOR) region extending southwards to the Equator. From the Straits of Hormuz in the West, it extends to the Straits of Malacca in the East.

Air Power Perspective

What is interesting from an air power perspective is that this entire region falls within the reach of a number of our combat ac in concert with existing force multipliers like FRA (Flight Refuelling Aircraft) and those on the anvil, like AWACS. In consonance with the IAF's transformation from a largely tactical air force to a strategic one with reach and precision strike capability, it is imperative that we start looking at 'intervention' and expeditionary capability that involves the entire range of air power capabilities in operations requiring surveillance, offensive action, extrication, peace enforcement and stabilisation. **In short, an air force with 'trans-oceanic strategic reach' is eminently suited to both projecting and protecting our interests — something that is the raison-de-etre of Out-of-Country Contingency operations.**

With the IAF emerging out of the closet, and transforming itself from a platform-intensive and tactically-oriented force to a technologically focussed force with strategic intervention capability, it is time to look at a significant role in any OCC. At a time when nations are hesitant to commit ground forces due to the 'body bag' effect, the ability of air power to engage strategic targets with minimum collateral damage, maximum effect and 'shape the battlefield' for swift operations by airborne assault or amphibious attack, has made it a preferred option in swift Out-of-Country conflict resolution, the likes of which were achieved in Kosovo. **While it is difficult to imagine any end state without a joint task force, the exponential advances in the IAF's Strike, sanitising and extrication capabilities must be taken into consideration while planning any Out-of-Country Contingencies.** Even when it comes to humanitarian intervention, it is the IAF's strategic mobility assets that have set the ball rolling for any of our interventions, be it during the tsunami or during the evacuation of Indian citizens from Iraq.

Raising the Stakes

India's increasing 'footprint' in the area means that it is only a matter of time before its influence spreads into Africa, CAR and SE Asia where it will continue to compete with China for resources and markets.[43] What this means is that Indian people and capital are likely to move into these relatively high-risk and unstable regions, in the hope that Government and military establishments are ready for 'intervention' and extrication at very short notice. What then should be the strategic aim of our Out-of-Country Contingency operations?

It should be "To support India's emergence as a global power by developing capabilities that assist intervention, extrication and coercion on foreign soil in furtherance of national security, economic and foreign policy objectives".

The next logical step would be to lay down clear-cut objectives to ensure that the strategic aim is swiftly executed without any ambiguity. These are:

- Define capabilities and work out realistic force structures.
- Identify existing and potential 'hot spots'.
- Facilitate inter-agency sharing of resources, manpower and intelligence by raising levels of inter-operability.
- Lay down an unambiguous and expeditious Command and Control structure that is based on a lean politico-military combination.
- Create gaming and mock situations to exercise available options.
- Sensitise the media and the public on the need to create such a capability.

Identifying Hot Spots

India's predicament in a fast-changing world order is manifold. 'Strategic Clarity' has not accompanied rapid globalisation and economic growth. Vulnerabilities

---

43   Kapil Kak, 'India–China Relations: An Overview', Air Power, *Journal of Air Power and Space Studies*, Vol. 3 Monsoon 2006.

of a 'Global India' have to be discussed to the most ridiculous levels of imagination, because that is what crisis is normally precipitated by. These 'hot spots' could be broadly classified under the following heads:

- Areas of interest and influence
- Areas of conflict
- Areas of fundamental divergence that threaten the fabric of the Indian state.

Under these broad classifications, some of the specific areas that can be identified based on existing geo-strategic realities and future assessments in no order of priority are highlighted below:

- Training camps of jehadi and fundamentalist non-state actors in PoK, Taliban-dominated areas of Afghanistan, and on our eastern borders.
- LTTE training camps in Sri Lanka, if they have the potential to threaten the fabric of our internal security mechanisms.
- Any threat by non-state actors to friendly littoral neighbours like Sri Lanka, the Maldives, Seychelles and even Madagascar.
- Threat to Indian strategic and economic infrastructure assets, like air bases in friendly foreign countries, oil rigs and large industrial plants.
- Any global hostage crisis involving Indian citizens.
- Humanitarian intervention following natural or induced disasters.
- WMD sites that have the potential to threaten national security.
- Enforcement of 'no fly zones' during pre-or post-hostilities phase.
- Follow-on operations in case any UN operation involving Indian forces is faced with insurmountable difficulties. In such a situation it is the duty of the Indian government to speedily intervene and support/extricate our forces.

Force Structure

The easiest thing to propound is to say, "Let us raise a Marine Corps with complete expeditionary capability". This is easier said than done in our 'limited resources scenario'. Brig. Gurmeet Kanwal (Retd.), a Senior Fellow at The Centre for Air Power Studies has articulated the broad need for creating a Rapid Reaction Division with two expeditionary assault Brigade Groups, one as an air assault brigade group, and the other as an amphibious brigade; however, no clear-cut command and control structure has yet been suggested.[44] What is

---

44   Brig. Gurmeet Kanwal (Retd.), 'Interventions Abroad', *The Tribune*, Chandigarh.

important here is the need to develop capability for simultaneous assault. A third brigade that is trained for air-landed induction as follow-on forces would complete the force structure. These formations would need to be self-sufficient in all respects and possess adequate fire power, mobility and sustainability for 3–4 weeks in varied terrain. Do we have the raw capability to put together such a force? The only grey areas presently are the composition of the amphibious assault and third follow-on brigade, and their associated airlift capability. A glaring omission in most suggested expeditionary force structures for India is the absence of any significant offensive air power assets being dovetailed into these formations. There is an urgent need to look closely at the IAF's strategic air power capability when it comes to putting together a Rapid Reaction Force. Some of the key missions of airpower other than those performed by integral helicopter assets of the Division during OCC are highlighted below:

- Strategic extrication of Indian nationals
- Enforcement of 'no fly zones' by Air Superiority Fighters
- Precision strikes as a means of shaping the battlefield
- Counter Surface Force Operations during both amphibious and airborne assault operations
- Combat support missions like AAR (Air–Air Refuelling), AWACS, Combat Search and Rescue and LRMP missions.

Typical surface forces assets for effective OCC would comprise:

- Special forces for small and localised interventions with suitable small insertion naval craft and suitable aerial platforms
- Specially trained brigade-size formations for airborne, air-landed and amphibious assault with adequate integral fire power
- Assault craft and fast attack craft
- Task force ships comprising a Carrier Battle Group (CBG) or a Heli-Carrier Group for sanitisation, fire support and show of force.

Aerial assets would broadly comprise:

- Two to four squadrons of multi-role combat aircraft and integral air from the CBG with maritime strike capability maybe the bare minimum that would be required to support a division strength force. Additionally, one integral Attack Helicopter squadron with the assault brigade and a Combat Search and Rescue element would be required. Needless to say, the quantum of heavy and medium-lift transport aircraft support to support such a large force during induction, sustenance and de-induction is well beyond our present capability of supporting a brigade-size airborne assault operation. This is an area crying for immediate attention if we are to create a credible OCC force.

Support Requirements for Effective Prosecution of Air Operations

Sustaining combined operations in general, and an air operation in particular, over thousands of kilometres in hostile territory is no easy task. The starting point for effective prosecution of air operations in OCC is highly precise, detailed and updated intelligence on a variety of targets. The next area of attention has to be to develop a string of 'transit corridors', turnaround or staging bases and 'contingency' bases. These, to a large extent, are dependent on our diplomatic finesse and capability. We need to develop and cultivate key partners in all our OCC contingencies. Networking for more effective Command and Control and maintaining a shorter sensor to shooter loop thousands of kilometres away is another key support requirement, as is the seamless integration of our newly integrated Logistics Management systems and operational data links. Sustainability of Out-of-Country Air Ops is only possible with a streamlined and highly responsive Combat Support System. Some of the critical issues relate to availability of centralized maintenance facilities, armament stores through a theatre distribution system that uses both commercial and military transport systems. These would include nodes very similar to those set up by the Coalition forces to support *Operation Desert Storm* and Iraqi Freedom. Assuming that a hypothetical OCC emerges on the East Coast of Africa or in the Middle East, we need to develop logistic corridors and identify bases in the Indian Ocean Region and North Africa to be able to effectively intervene and sustain operations. Politico-diplomatic-Military operations have to be so closely synergised that the operation goes through like the Entebbe raid.

Management of OCC Operations

One of the most comprehensive documents on 'Managing Complex Contingencies' abroad was brought out by the US in the form of a Presidential Decision Directive (PDD) in 1997.[45] Seeing the complexity of the post-Cold War world environment, it was correctly realised that military missions would get more and complicated and veer away from the 'predictable' to the 'unpredictable and nebulous'. There was a realisation that real soldiering and clean war fighting

---

45 *Managing Complex Contingency Operations*, US PDD, 1997.

missions were gradually being replaced by military operations other than War (MOOW) in remote and hostile parts of the world.[46] The paper defines 'Complex Contingency Operations' as peace operations such as the peace accord implementation operation conducted by NATO in Bosnia (1995-present) and the humanitarian intervention in northern Iraq called *Operation Provide Comfort* (1991); and foreign humanitarian assistance operations, such as *Operation Support Hope* in central Africa (1994) and *Operation Sea Angel* in Bangladesh (1991). Unless otherwise directed, this PDD does not apply to domestic disaster relief or to relatively routine or small-scale operations, nor to military operations conducted in defence of US citizens, territory, or property, including counter-terrorism and hostage-rescue operations and international armed conflict. The document, while acknowledging the importance of international and regional organisations without actually naming them, does not relinquish the capability to respond unilaterally.

What is important is to note that this PDD was good camouflage for military interventions by US and coalition forces. What then are the key take-aways from this document that would help us in clearly articulating ourselves in this area? Management of the politico-diplomatic-military process lies at the epicentre of the OCC plan. The OODA loop for this kind of contingency in our context is presently unacceptably slow and needs immediate streamlining. Some of the key issues that need to be addressed are:

- Speedy situation assessments based on multiple intelligence inputs (IB, RAW, MI and diplomatic inputs) are imperative. The assessment should look at four critical issues.
- Does the situation threaten Indian interests — immediate or future? Is an intervention necessary and is it possible? What are the possible ramifications? What is the desired end state?
- A clear mission statement and key politico-military objectives should flow clearly out of the situation assessment. The concept of operations with clear inter-agency roles and lead agency responsibilities must be defined.
- Crisp operational and support plans with comprehensive training, rehearsals and regular combat orientation must be carried out with clear politico-military exit strategies laid down, unlike the quagmire of Iraq.
- Deliberate after-action reviews and debriefs must be carried out to assess inter-agency planning, coordination and execution. Lessons learnt must thereafter be swiftly disseminated to relevant agencies.

---

46 Anthony Zinni, 'A Military for the 21st Century: Lessons from the Past', at the Joint Forces Staff College, May 24, 2001.

The United Nations and the Way Ahead

One of the main reasons for powerful nations like the USA, China, and the NATO countries to plan unilateral or multi-lateral OCC operations is the abysmal failure of UN-led interventions in 'hot spots' the world over. The absence of a clear charter for intervention and the reluctance to use force to 'get a situation under control' has meant that a 'passive presence' in the form of peace-keeping missions, and ineffective peace enforcement missions have led to extreme cynicism about the UN's capability to restore order in an increasingly dangerous and fragmented world. It is very clear that the UN in its present state and without the necessary mandate, is incapable of protecting a sovereign state's overseas economic interests and citizens. It is also incapable of preventing terror strikes and genocides sparked by religious fundamental elements. Why then should a powerful and emerging global power like India not prepare itself in every way to protect its strategic interests on its own, or with countries with converging interests and common threats? Does not China openly advocate its preparedness for planning for 'contingencies' in Taiwan and beyond its immediate periphery?[47] This does not in any way dilute India's commitment to supporting humanitarian interventions by the UN; it is just that our capabilities and concerns have forced us to widen our options without being apologetic any more. The past few years have seen the Indian armed forces train with a number of modern army, naval and air forces. These exercises have provided valuable preliminary lessons in understanding inter-operability issues and mindsets. We need to move on to the next level of identifying partners for a possible multilateral intervention in hot spots. This is not going to be an easy task and would warrant a tightrope politico-military balancing act.

Organisational Issues

The present organisation for OCC is very loosely structured with the Crisis Management Group within the Cabinet Committee on Security (CCS) being the apex decision-making authority. In the absence of any integrated defence organisation or theatre commands, it is imperative that all OCC forces be placed under Command of SFC. The air element for this force structure would cater to three scenarios, viz. Air-Land, Air Maritime and Tri-Service contingencies. The next issue relates to Command and Control issues. Presently, all these assets are under individual service/command HQs. Who would command and control

---

47   Ibid. Note, Kapil Kak.

these forces in an OCC? In the absence of a viable Theatre Command concept it is imperative that some kind of structure is put in place! A workable short-term measure would be to place all forces under the command of C-in-C, Strategic Forces Command with Operational responsibility resting with a JFC (Joint Forces Cdr) who would typically be a Major General/Lieutenant General or equivalent rank from the other services with individual component commanders being Brigadier/Major General or equivalent. In case of a predominantly maritime option, the JFC could be a two/three-star Admiral, and if it is a predominantly land-oriented scenario, a two/three-star General could be the JFC. All air assets, irrespective of whether they are shore based or ship based, would be under op control of the JFACC (Joint Force Air Component Commander) with maritime forces being under command of the JFNC. A lean command and control structure is depicted below:

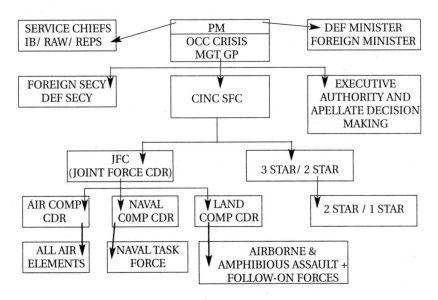

Success and Failure — A Historical Perspective

A critical analysis of a number of Out-of-Area interventions by a number of countries reveals that air power has played a significant role in facilitating the end state in most situations. Conversely, incorrect or inadequate use of air power has seen various conflicts dragging on for years. Vietnam is a classic case in point where incorrect use of air power resulted in escalation, widespread international condemnation and steeling of the resolve of the Vietnam Congress to achieve their objectives. The stunning nuclear strike by the Israelis over Osirak, reduced in one stroke, the looming nuclear threat to the very existence of the Israeli state. The audacious long-distance strike missions over Libya came as a timely rejoinder to Gadaffi to mend his ways. High stakes and immediate threats are two major reasons for launching unilateral or multilateral coalition operations, with or without UN approval. Typical examples are the IPKF operations, NATO operations during Allied Force and Coalition operations against Saddam Hussein. While the Indian Peace Keeping Force (IPKF) intervention in Sri Lanka did give India valuable experience in Out-of-Country interventions, the cost it paid in terms of casualties was too high for comfort. While there are many reasons for the limited success of the IPKF operations, prime amongst them were poor inter-agency synergy, poor planning, conflicting intelligence pictures and the reluctance to use air power offensively, which left the ground forces to fight with 'one hand tied behind their backs'. It is certain that accurate intelligence coupled with air strikes to support the ill-fated Jaffna University heli-borne operation, would have broken the LTTE's back. Both *Operation Pawan* (Sri Lanka) and *Operation Cactus* (Maldives) — the former, a limited success and the latter, a total success, are classic examples of how OCC ought not to be planned. The success of the US-led coalition air attacks on Serbian forces forced Milosevic on to the negotiating table without committing any ground forces.[48] The third largest air operation since World War II after *Vietnam* and *Desert Storm, Operation Allied Force* over Kosovo was a classic case of coalition air operations in an Out-of-Country Contingency situation with numerous inter-agency conflicts, yet it was able to achieve the 'desired end state', viz. the removal of Milosevic. The operation was fraught with inter-operability problems between NATO countries and the US, hesitant targeting, and excessive political interference that mostly related to mitigating the risks of collateral damaged and loss of innocent lives. What saved the day was good intelligence and copious use of PGMs that permitted EBO (Effects-based Operations). It was very clear in *Operation Allied Force* over Kosovo that technology showed the way for air power to play the lead role in an OCC operation and showcase the emerging potential of air power in speedy conflict resolution.[49] While such an operation cannot be used as a template for all OCC (Israel was taught a bitter lesson in Lebanon), it serves a reminder of the potent capability of air power to shape events hundreds and thousands of miles away. Historically, if one looks at the last four decades, there has been an increase in the number and intensity of complex contingencies that have warranted military interventions; Somalia, Rwanda, Haiti, and Bosnia, to name just a few. This trend is only going to increase, hence the importance to be well prepared.

---

48 Benjamin Lambeth, *Air War Over Kosovo*, Rand Project Air Force.
49 Ibid.

War Gaming and Exercises

While war-gaming and exercises are important to hone skills in any kind of warfare, it assumes even greater importance in OCC. This is primarily to enable the force to penetrate the 'fog of war' that is likely to be thicker in alien territory, and against unpredictable foes, something that is reduced in conventional engagements.[50] In early 2000, the Pentagon conceived a situational analysis and war game called the Millennium Challenge that pitted a conventional expeditionary force with all its technological might against a rogue military commander who broke away from his government somewhere in the Persian Gulf and threatened the very fabric of peace in the region.[51] A dynamic retired General, known for his intellectual brilliance and 'out-of-the-box' thinking methods was chosen to play the 'rogue commander'. Not very happy with the conventional manner in which *Op Desert Storm* was fought, and sensing that the US had to prepare itself for 'bloody unconventional engagements', this exercise was conceived even before 9/11 happened. The results of Round 1 of the exercise, that was finally held in 2002 after almost two years of detailed planning were startling with the rogue commander's 'Red force' inflicting very heavy and unacceptable losses on the Blue force.[52] Coming as it did in the wake of 9/11 and USA's declared war on terror, it proved decisive in beefing up their OCC plans, which were finally put into practice during *Operation Iraqi Freedom* and *Operation Enduring Freedom*. India is surrounded by potentially failed states that could descend into chaos and cause peripheral damage to India. What prevents Prabhakaran from seizing complete control of the northern part of Sri Lanka? What if Prachanda and his Maoists plunge Nepal into anarchy? Does Bangladesh have the potential to go the Taliban way? What if the Taliban regains control of Afghanistan and renews the practice of pushing foreign mercenaries into J&K? What if Musharraf is overthrown by fundamentalists and PoK becomes a haven for cross-border terrorism again — are we going to react passively? These and many more are highly probable scenarios that need to be gamed for OCC operations if we are to be prepared for any eventuality and break out of the mould of being perceived as a 'soft state' that is incapable of responding to attacks on its sovereignty. Planning and gaming an appropriate 'exit strategy' is one of the most important ingredients of a viable OCC plan, a critical blunder made by the Bush administrationduring *Operation Iraqi Freedom*. It is also very important for the military to have a major say in exit contingency planning as

---

50 William Owens, *Lifting the Fog of War*, Farrar Strauss, 2000.
51 Malcolm Gladwel, *Blink*, Penguin Books, 2006 pp. 95–106.
52 Ibid.

troop fatigue, media intrusion and other psychological aspects of international pressure are likely to degrade the war waging potential of the deployed units, just as it did in Vietnam.

Pitfalls and Roadblocks

In the present scenario, if there is a prime area of concern, it is the gross inadequacy of air mobility assets for strategic intervention. Something needs to be done fast if the IAF's potent strategic strike capability is not complemented by adequate strategic mobility. Translating this into action, we need to ask ourselves — if we have to launch brigade-size airborne and amphibious assault operations, preceded by 'Strategic Strike operation on a target between 1500 and 3000 km away, do we have the strategic mobility assets to support all the operations, considering that the strike ac may have to 'turn around' at a remote but friendly base? The answer would be an emphatic No, considering that the IL-76 is the only platform that can perform the role at the distances envisaged. Even if we manage to put together a string of support and logistic nodes enroute to the conflict area, where are the medium-lift aircraft of the An-32 or C-130 Hercules class to support such operations?

The IAF has one dedicated Maritime Strike Squadron that could also train for OCC. How do we train a few other multi-role squadrons for OCC Operations with an ability to speedily adapt to alien airspace, long duration missions and varied threats? Moving down the chain, another tricky issue relates to identifying ground formations for OCC. No major problems are envisaged when it comes to committing troops for airborne assault. Problems would arise when it comes to putting together amphibious assault and follow-on forces. Would the troops be drawn from our strike corps formations, trained periodically during peacetime and revert to their parent formations? Or, do we need to raise an exclusive amphibious assault brigade and not just a brigade that is comfortable in 'watery battlefields' and locate it suitably? The latter seems the most viable option, but do we have the resources? Joint tactics would have to be developed and honed up to levels where failure is unacceptable. How is that possible when we don't even have an establishment to develop joint tactics for conventional operations? How do we tackle turf battles during peace-time training schedules? Ensuring that our multiple Intelligence agencies put their act together and provide accurate intelligence is also going to be a Herculean task. How do we ensure that the Sri Lanka and Kargil experiences are not repeated? Imagine if the opposition at Male during *Operation Cactus* had been even marginal. Would any casualties have been expected and accepted? These questions and many more have to be answered before we can put together a potent and well-trained OCC Task Force. Changing mindsets is another key area when it comes to tackling OCC. In all probability, OCC operations are mainly going to be launched mainly against non-state actors who are adept at unconventional, spontaneous and unscrupulous war-fighting techniques. Is our leadership at all levels ready to cast aside their conservative, dogmatic and highly predictable manner of functioning, and recognise the need for radical and 'out-of-the-box' thinking and tactics? Media and public sensitisation is another critical area, especially when it comes to OCC operations. Accepting casualties in military operations, be it conventional or operations other than war within the confines of our own geographical boundaries has rarely been a problem. Translate the same to operations overseas where the common man does not understand 'national interests, and what you have is furore and public indignation and the cry to 'get the boys back home'. This phenomenon itself is reason enough to build strong air power intervention capability. Keeping with India's emergence as a responsible power, protection of our strategic national interests should be the sole guiding factor of any Out-of-Country Contingency doctrine, and certainly, it must not be interventionist in nature.

Summary

Having looked at almost the entire spectrum of Out-of-Country Contingency operations, it would be appropriate, even at the cost of repetition, to list certain imperatives for putting together a doctrine, raising a viable force and ensuring inter-operability. These are:

- Identification of areas of interest, concern and conflict, leading to identification of 'hot spots'
- Politico-diplomatic-military convergence on the need for Out-of-Country intervention capability
- Consensus on force structure, command, control, intelligence and inter-operability issues
- Recognition of air power as a major component of OCC that can effectively contribute to the shaping of the battlefield, speedy conflict resolution and reducing attrition
- Realistic training and war gaming to include interoperability with other countries with similar perceptions on threats and intervention and end states with viable exit strategies.

JOINTMANSHIP — TRAINING AND MINDSET — THE KEYS TO SYNERGY IN THE COMBINED ARMS CONCEPT

From the days of the Burma Campaign and the airlift of 1 Sikh into Srinagar in 1947, to the synergistic attacks on Karachi, capture of Dacca in December 1971 and victory on the icy heights of Kargil, Jointmanship or the Combined Arms concept is nothing new for the Indian armed forces. India was first off the block when it came to setting up 'joint institutions' of training and learning, like the NDA and DSSC, models that are being replicated the world over. With a legacy as strong as this, India should have led the way when it came to developing synergies and maximizing its combat potential. What has happened instead, is a realization that, in an era where economic progress has overshadowed military might, budgetary constraints and public/media scrutiny have forced large armed forces like that of India to introspect and see how they can extract more 'bang for the buck'. This is but one of the many compulsions that has pushed the 'jointmanship' dilemma into the forefront. Recent conflicts in the Falklands, Gulf and Afghanistan have shown that true jointmanship goes well beyond the 'Airland Battle' concept and single-service capabilities are being joined together weeks or months before a 'crunch or conflict' situation. It also transcends beyond the skin-deep understanding that we presently possess each other's capabilities and limitations. To say that we are on the wrong track is to belittle the tremendous effort made over the last five decades; however, to introspect and effect a mid-course change is no crime, in fact, it is an absolute necessity.

The recently published 'Joint Doctrine of the Indian Armed Forces' mostly articulates what we already know and steers clear of any radical and far-reaching changes, especially where it deals with 'Operational Imperatives for Change'. It is conservative, circumspect of being critical of shortfalls and does not articulate a concrete methodology of how we need to adopt the suggested model. To be absolutely fair, what it has certainly done is to act as a catalyst for debate on how to improve synergies and move from 'Jointmanship' to a truly Combined Arms Concept. If one were to simplistically highlight the three vital ingredients of Jointmanship, they would be Training, Mindset and Joint Operational Art. All three are closely interlinked and complement each other in an open loop. There are no better practitioners of Operational Art worldwide than Generals, Admirals and Air Marshals of the Indian armed forces. The tactical acumen of formation commanders of all the three services is what has propelled India to the world centre-stage as far as joint exercises are concerned, with numerous countries waiting in queue. What then is impeding the progress in areas related to jointmanship, interoperability and synergy arming the three Services? Is it the other two compartments, viz. training and mindset?

This article would attempt to introspect and reflect on two imperatives, viz. Training and Mindset, which are vital for propelling jointmanship to new levels and harnessing synergies to cope with the existing realities and paradigms of warfare. Some of the questions asked would be:

- Is our focus on joint training superficial and 'skin deep'? Is it more about control of ideas and assets rather than harnessing and exploiting them?
- Are our mindsets too conservative, rigid, and are we, at times, oblivious of the rapid changes overtaking militaries the world over?
- Is there a dichotomy between what is articulated and what is practised? Are we not concentrating too much on a 'top–down approach' to jointmanship'?

Building Blocks of Jointmanship

The Induction Phase Less than 50 per cent of the officer intake into the armed forces in India is from the NDA, a figure that is significantly lower as compared to 10 years ago, owing to the inability of NDA to cope with the rapid expansion of the armed forces. As a result of this, a large number of officers from the three services, many of them from the fighting arms, is exposed to very little Joint Training until they meet their counterparts from the other services at DSSC, Wellington. By then, mindsets have been developed and joint concepts are more in theory and less in practice, with single-service concepts dominating the entire thought cycle of future staff officers and commanders. What are the options available to set this right? Some are:

- Expand NDA to ensure that all graduate-level intakes into the armed forces are through the NDA. Postgraduate intake into technical and specialized streams must go through a Joint Services capsule at the NDA prior to commissioning. Even the existing syllabi at NDA needs to be bolstered by more joint service academic content that is pitched at the right level.
- If the above is not possible, all non ex NDA officers must be put through a Joint Services YOs (young officers) capsule with both individual service and joint service content.

Early Years

The early years of training are, understandably, characterized by intense single-service skill accumulation. At ground level, it is a phase of undesirable isolation from tactical concepts of 'joint war fighting'. Senior leadership is firm in their conviction that focus and acquisition of individual service professional knowledge is far more important than acquiring knowledge of the other services. Keeping in mind the rapid advances in technology and the ongoing revolution in military affairs, we need to look at it from a different perspective, wherein we build up joint war-fighting capability during the early years of service; capability that is capable of swift intervention in scenarios as diverse as Low-Intensity Conflict Operations, Counter-Insurgency Ops, Protection of Maritime interests and Multinational Force interventions, all of which we are currently undertaking. Some thoughts on enhancing interoperability and jointmanship for officers between 3 and 8 years of service are:-

- Commencement of a Joint Junior Commanders' Course for all officers of the three services that is merit based and pitched at the tactical level, the aim being to create a pool of officers who are jointly trained and tactically aware at the battalion, squadron and ship levels.
- A specific Junior Combat Commanders' Course can also be conducted to identify and nurture tactically proficient officers from the fighting arms of the three services who would go on years later to refine and hone joint war fighting tactics, strategy and doctrine.
- Selected officers from all branches and streams could also be sent on cross attachments for 3–6 months at the Battalion, Squadron and Warship level with a clear mandate of what to assimilate and take back.

The Middle Years (12–25 years)

This is a period wherein the Indian armed forces devote the maximum time towards discussing and understanding joint war-fighting tactics at institutions like the Defence Services Staff College, and attempt to move up the value chain during the three Higher Command Courses. In the present context, this is rather late as the bulk of the joint syllabi at DSSC is devoted to understanding tactics of the other services, something that should have been done much earlier, probably at the Junior Commanders' Course. Without blindly aping some other countries who have redesigned the content at their Staff Colleges to make it more responsive to present and emerging challenges, we too need to look very closely at overhauling the training methodology at our staff college and decide whether it is time to do away with three separate Higher Command Courses, and replace it with a single one. As a representative example, if one looks very honestly at the training syllabi at DSSC, the basic framework, content, methodologies and composition of Directing Staff has remained relatively unchanged over the last three decades, with only cosmetic changes having been effected in terms of addition and deletion of various packages. Some random joint training-related issues as food for thought are as follows:

- Review the entire syllabus at DSSC to make it truly joint in all respects throughout the course after only an initial period of single service re-orientation, focussing more on operational art, strategy and doctrine as against the present 'tactical heavy content'. This would be possible only if tactical proficiency is honed at the junior command and unit levels.
- Moving up the value chain in terms of content will enable staff officers and potential commanders to understand the implication and process of joint capabilities, strategy and doctrine as articulated by their formation commanders. It will also teach them to exercise greater initiative and independent decision-making.
- Eight to ten years later, meeting up again, albeit in lesser numbers and sharing a common platform at a common Higher Command course will offer tremendous potential to look back critically and analytically at years, events and operations gone by. This would, inevitably, form the final building blocks before attitudes, operational experiences and perceptions get translated into doctrine and policy. Can it go wrong? In all probability not, since the architects would have cut their teeth, trained, fought, led and taught together.

The Senior Years

Offering an opinion on mindsets, attitudes and perceptions of our seniors is an extremely daunting proposition, made even more difficult when it relates to an issue as sensitive as jointmanship. What makes it a trifle easier is that the leadership in all three services acknowledge that there are roadblocks on the 'Combined Arms' route. They also acknowledge that 'turf' battles and mindsets act as major impediments to jointmanship. What are the main areas of conflict that need to be resolved as seen from the middle level? Some of them are:

- Fear/apprehension of losing resources, vacancies, control and power
- Reluctance to look at the 'big picture' or national and global realities, and

look only at parochial individual service interest, the mantra being 'protect service interests and then only fit in joint imperatives'

- A distinct reluctance to accept the changed nature of warfare, its uncertainty, speed and variety. While the old adage, 'Victory is measured by foot' still rings true, so is the exponentially lethal and swift impact of air power on conflict resolution, with minimum loss of life and destruction. Energy interests and trade are vital for a nation's survival, and who better than maritime forces to project and protect these vital interests.

International Perspectives

At a symposium at the National Defence University, in January 2002, US Secretary of Defence Donald Rumsfeld remarked, "The lesson of the war in Afghanistan is that effectiveness in Combat will depend heavily on jointness and how well the different branches of the military can communicate and coordinate their efforts on the battlefield. Achieving that jointness in wartime requires building that jointness in peacetime. We need to train like we fight and fight like we train and, too often, we don't". "Prophetic words indeed because soon after, the US-led coalition forces unleashed a simultaneous combined arms campaign to remove Saddam Hussein from power during *Operation Iraqi Freedom*. The campaign was as different from the one prosecuted during *Desert Storm* as 'chalk is from cheese', the main difference being the simultaneity in attack and speed of execution that was only made possible because of Secretary Rumsfeld's insistence on jointness, inter-operability and synergy at every level. Presently, military technology has overtaken military thinking and therein lies part of the problem. Aerospace and naval power are heavily technology intensive and form vital components of the technology that has overtaken thinking. An appreciation of this would go a long way in bridging 'mindsets' as they exist today in terms of understanding each other's capabilities and shaping realistic joint warfare strategies for the future. The US Army is defining a new joint operational architecture that is going to integrate seamlessly with the emerging strike capability of US air and naval forces. Joint doctrine the world over is being shaped by technology and 'effect'-based compulsions. Given the predominance of the Indian Army in post-Independence operations, integration of new and emerging capabilities of air and naval forces is proving to be a bit of a stumbling block and one of the impediments in putting together an operationally viable 'Combined Arms Doctrine'. It is said that the wise learn from others' mistakes, while the foolish are condemned to repeat them — nowhere is it more apt than in our quest for 'jointness'. During the days of the classical Airland Battle, defining Joint Force capability was not a very difficult task for commanders. This is probably why the easiest thing to do is to quote Montgomery and Churchill and question as to why it is so difficult to evolve Joint Doctrines today. The answer lies in the absence of clearly identifiable enemies, making it extremely difficult to lay out joint warfighting tactics that spread across the spectrum of conflict. The Army will continue to say that barring an odd Kosovo example, conflicts are ultimately decided by a nations ability to occupy and hold ground; proponents of airpower will say that the enemy is a system and only air power can reach the 'heart of the system' by systematically targeting 'Centres of Gravity, and the Navy will assert that our global and regional ambitions hinge on our ability to dominate the Sea Lines of Communications (SLOCs) and project maritime power.

THE BUILDING BLOCKS OF JOINTMANSHIP

INDUCTION PHASE	- NDA
	- JT SERVICES' CAPSULE
	- JT YOUNG OFFICERS' CAPSULE
EARLY YEARS	- JUNIOR COMMAND
	- JUNIOR COMBAT COMMAND
	- CROSS TRAINING
MIDDLE YEARS	- JOINT STAFF COURSE
	- JOINT HIGHER COMMAND
SENIOR YEARS	- NATIONAL DEFENCE COLLEGE
DESIRED END STATE	- CHANGED MINDSET AT SENIOR LEADERSHIP LEVELS AND POTENT JOINT WARFIGHTING CAPABILITY

There is a distinct difference between 'Joint Training' and 'Training Jointly'. While the former is like a well-composed painting with no rough edges, the latter is like a jigsaw puzzle in which joint players are desperately trying to fit in the pieces till the last moment. It needs very little imagination to decide which model is to be followed. In the Indian context, geopolitical imperatives, topography and preponderance of low intensity/counter-insurgency/urban warfare conflict scenarios would ensure that the army's role would not diminish in any way. However, the emergence of political and strategic preferences for 'effect-based operations' against centres of gravity and coercive diplomacy as a speedy means of conflict resolution has catapulted air power to the forefront as a vital component of military power. India's maritime interests, international forays in search of fast-depleting energy resources and protection of SLOCs makes it imperative for us to focus adequately on maritime forces. We need to look beyond mere budgetary allocations and control of various commands, and embrace jointness with speed and a 'spirit of give and take'. This is possible only if we adopt a parallel approach of tackling organisational changes from the top and initiating simultaneous changes in training patterns from the 'bottom'. There can be no better way to sign off than by reiterating what Maj. Gen. Jatinder Singh (Retd.) articulated in an article written in October 2005. He wrote: "Jointness has to be accepted as reality. We are moving too slowly in modernising the training and technology used in joint missions. It is time to shake ourselves out of this professional morass of individual service cultures and realise the potential and importance of each service for various tasks". At the end of the day, we have to realise that if the three services cannot resolve jointmanship issues, force restructuring would ultimately be dictated by politics in a democracy, just as the way it was done in the US and UK. The sooner we realise this, the smoother will be the transition to true jointness.

This article was published in the inaugural issue of *The Purple Pages* — a professional military journal brought out by HQ Integrated Defence Staff.

CHINA'S WHITE PAPER ON DEFENCE — DECEMBER 2004 AN 'INDIA-CENTRIC' ANALYSIS

The biggest dilemma facing the Indian strategic community is to identify the space that China occupies in our threat perception. Some questions that are fuelling continuous debate in our country relate to China's realignment of its military force structure and the ensuing ramifications on the strategic balance in the region.

Raison d'être for White Papers

It is remarkable that during the period of 2000-2005, when India had not even managed to put together a Joint Doctrine, leave alone publish a White Paper on National Defence, China came up with four White Papers on defence. These papers clearly articulate the country's hopes, ambitions and seek to cement a firm slot in the comity of nations as a power to reckon with over the next century. The basic aim of a White Paper is to clearly articulate a nation's strategic thinking in any discipline with a two-fold aim. The primary aim is to provide a basic framework and clear political directions in critical areas that are likely to have a direct impact on the 'Grand Strategy of a Nation'. The secondary aim of the paper is to share a country's assessment of its environment, capabilities and aspirations with an international audience.[53] White Papers are normally published when geopolitical changes are imminent in any critical discipline, like the economy or defence and is likely to impinge on a number of directly and indirectly related areas. A classic example is the South African White Paper on defence that came out a few years after the dismantling of apartheid. It was extremely critical for the South African Government to indicate to the people and the international community that far-reaching changes were imminent in the composition of the defence forces and threat perceptions. It was also meant to assuage the fears of the 'white minority' that they would be victimized, and at the same time spell out a framework and time frame for smooth transfer of command, authority, responsibility and expertise to the black majority. The White Paper has gone a long way in ensuring a smooth changeover with minimum conflict and is primarily a result of the vision and statesmanship of

---

53   Senior Col Chen Zhou, Expert Deciphers White Paper on National Defence, *People's Daily*, 13 December 2002.

Mr. Nelson Mandela and Mr. Thabo Mbeki. So, what were the main catalysts for a quick succession of White Papers on Defence from the PRC? The first has to be the rapid change in the nature of warfare the world over and the Chinese realization that the ongoing RMA is an inescapable reality. More specifically, the White Paper clearly seeks to dispel the classic image of the Chinese armed forces as being reliant on 'mass and mechanization' and shift focus on to its transformation into a technology-intensive force that is preparing for informationalized warfare.[54] The emergence of the US as the sole superpower has clearly irked the Chinese and the paper clearly spells out the need for a more equitable world order with the PLA as a key instrument of this change. Lastly, the paper heralds the handing over of the baton of overall responsibility of the PLA from Mr. Jiang Zemin to Mr. Hu Jintao, signalling the end of the Deng era and the beginning of a new one with technocrats and professionals at the helm of affairs.

The entire White Paper is divided into ten chapters as given below and all the chapters would be discussed keeping in mind an 'India-centric' perspective.

The Security Situation
National Defence Policy
RMA with Chinese Characterstics
Defence Expenditure and Defence Assets
The Military Service System
National Defence Mobilization and Reserve Force Building
Science Technology and Industry for National Defence
The Armed Forces and the People
International Security Cooperation
Arms Control Disarmament and Non Proliferation

International Security Situation

The PRC, while acknowledging that the present international situation is in a state of flux, clearly points at the beginning of a struggle for strategic points, strategic resources and strategic dominance. From the Chinese point of view, strategic resources mainly imply energy resources that stretch from Kazakhakistan and Iran to Angola, Sudan, Canada and Cuba. Strategic points are those points that control the flow of these resources, key amongst them being the Malacca Straits and African waters apart from the Central Asian Republics, and strategic dominance focuses on dominating or influencing territory, communication lanes and even

---

54   Ibid.

the mindsets of people and countries that compete for or facilitate the availability of these resources. Other than the Taiwanese obsession, China appears to have no ambitions of territorial expansion. The few territorial disputes that it has with Russia, Japan and India are likely to be resolved in order to focus on two main issues that are clearly articulated. These are:

- Checkmating Taiwanese attempts at Constitutional independence and working towards peaceful reunification failing which, be prepared for a military solution
- Equipping themselves in every way to challenge the 'Sole Superpower' status of the United States.

National Defence Policy

No nation that aspires to achieve superpower status and power projection over thousands of kilometres can hope to achieve that goal with a purely defensive strategy. At the same time, an overtly aggressive strategy as adopted by 'fundamentalist' nations or groups runs the risk of international isolation and condemnation. Keeping with Chinese tradition of deeply thought-out strategy, the PLA has been tasked with adopting a Strategy of 'Active Defence' that leaves enough room for manoeuvre and corresponds very closely to the 'Bush doctrine' that calls for elimination of threats to 'American democracy' as close to its roots as possible. While the Chinese Strategy is not as explicit, it is very clear that the Chinese Armed Forces are preparing themselves for active 'global intervention' in areas that the PRC has a direct or indirect influence.

RMA with Chinese Characteristics

A whole chapter is devoted to RMA with Chinese characteristics which indicate that the Chinese have been very systematic and measured in their response to RMA and not blindly aped the west, something that India needs to take note of. It has taken the Chinese almost ten years to articulate themselves on how they plan to adapt to RMA and it is through clear-cut political directives that it has been done keeping in mind all the strategic objectives and economic compulsions. Most important, it has stuck to the ideological objectives of a Communist society. Some of the the key features are highlighted below:

- Speedy transition from mechanization and mass to informationalization
- **Shift in focus from the PLA to the Navy, Air Force and Second Artillery force**
  A planned reduction of PLA by 200,000 to 2.3 million troops by end-2005

would allow this shift in focus. Restructuring the ratio between officers and men by reducing the number of officers and assigning more responsibility to SNCOs is also a KRA, as is improving leadership and command structures by compressing command chains and reducing office functions.

- **Concept of 'Active Defence'** On the one hand the Chinese talk vaguely about active defence but on the other hand, they are seeking to enhance their capabilities to win command of the sea, command of the air and to conduct strategic counter strikes. While the strengthening of the PLA Second Artillery force, a force tasked with nuclear counter attacks and precision strikes with conventional missiles as a deterrent component and the strengthening of the PLA Navy to 'protect' the sovereignty of its territorial seas and maritime interests as deterrent components are understandable as part of an 'Active Defence Strategy', it is the dichotomy in its 'air strategy' that exposes the aggressive intent in Chinese military strategy. On the one hand, the paper talks about "Efforts to build a defensive Air Force that possess integrated systems and a complete array of information support and operational means", and on the other, it talks about "Command of the Air". The fact of the matter lies in that by 2010 the PLAAF would have in its inventory over 300 SU-30 and Su-27 aircraft, whose role would certainly not be only to pursue 'active AD'.[55]

- **Implementation of the Strategic Project for Talented People** A drive to harness scientific, technological and strategic talent with long-term aims has been put in place. More and more military personnel will be trained by regular institutions of higher learning for both military and civilian use. In a key project called Project for Strengthening the Military with High Calibre Personnel, 30 regular institutions of higher learning have been identified to train personnel in key dual-purpose disciplines. The plan appears to be much focused and well planned.

- Reformation of the armed forces personnel to tune them to reality and bring them out of the closet that they have been for the last five decades.

- **Military Cooperation** A significant increase has been seen in military cooperation with countries with 'similar objectives' to promote inter-operability and trust. The large-scale manoeuvres held by China with Russia earlier this year within the framework of the SCO (Shanghai Cooperation Organisation) are clear indicators of this objective. Kazakhastan, Uzbekisan, Krygistan and Tajikistan are other members of the organisation, with India as an observer. Though the focus is on preventing and combating terrorism, it is

---

55   Richard Fisher, Jr, PLAAF Equipment Trends, NDU Conference "PLA and Chinese Society in Transition", 30 October 2001.

also a clear signal to the US that the Central Asian region is being watched carefully by China.

- **Integral Logistic Management** Considering the size of the PRC and multiple fronts to be manned very much like India, a need was felt for a Tri-Service Integrated Logistics command in every theatre. Medical and logistics outsourcing has also been accelerated.
- **Nation Building** Just as the Indian armed forces contribute significantly to nation building and assist the government during natural calamities, the PLA additionally attaches great significance to ideological and cultural work to preserve and further Marxism-Leninism, Mao Zedong Thought and Deng Xiaoping Theory.

Defence Expenditure

Some key numbers of Chinese defence expenditure indicate that annual defence expenditure has increased from 1.09 per cent of GDP in 1997 to 1.85 per cent in 2004 and is exponentially lower than that of the US and significantly lower than those of France, UK and even Japan. The official Chinese defence budget for 2004-05 was 211 billion yuan or almost 26 billion US dollar as against India's defence budget of US$ 16 billion for 2005-2006, which is 2.5 per cent of the Indian GDP. An increase of 14 per cent was predicted for 2005-2006, making it close to US $29.6 Billion, making it almost twice the Indian defence budget. Western analysts have pegged the Chinese defence budget for 2005-2006 as being closer to 6–8 per cent of GDP and considering that financial disclosures, have always been a weak area with Chinese financial articulations, these amount to a massive increase in defence expenditure, mainly focusing on RMA assets and makes the PLA the third best funded armed force after the US and Russia as against Chinese claims in the paper that even Japan, UK and France spend more on defence. This figure does not also include arms purchases and weapons research and development. A Rand Corporation report on Chinese defence expenditure indicates a 2025 defence budget of US$ 185 billion based on 2001 valuations and considers a conservative annualised growth rate of 5 per cent in GDP, a figure that is likely to be exceeded at least for the next 5 years before growth slows down. An interesting aspect of the White Paper is that special mention has been made of budgetary reform, the improvement of tendering and bidding systems for procurement and centralized payment of defence materials projects and services. This clearly points at attempts to usher in transparency in what was supposedly a corrupt and closed system. An earlier White Paper in 2002 had acknowledged that though the defence spending relative to state financial spending had reduced from 17.37 per cent in 1979 to 7.65 in 2001[56] actual expenditure had increased manifold because of the spectacular growth of the economy and rise in GDP. If one compares the two White Papers of 2002 and 2004, there do appear certain contradictions that clearly indicate camouflaging of real expenditure, an exercise that is even carried out by transparent western economies like the US and Japan. Western analysts also opine that actual Chinese defence expenditure is between 2–3[57] times the projected figure, which works out to US$ 52–78 billion for 2004-05, three times India's defence budget for 2005-2006 at the lower end and almost five times at the upper end. As the Chinese economy reaches the peak of its growth cycle around 2010-2015, there are bound to be major hiccups in terms of uncontrolled budget deficit and pressures to divert funds to other areas, prime amongst them being the social security sector, education and healthcare sectors. This is bound to impinge on defence spending and a major reappraisal of Chinese defence expenditure may have to be undertaken during this period.

Military Service System

Active Service

The PRC practises a direct and unambiguous system of military service that comprises conscripts and volunteers as part of the active force and a militia with reservists. Active servicemen include officers, soldiers and civil cadres. The officers are recruited from graduate schools, institutions of higher learning, military academies and outstanding soldiers. The rank structure is the same for all three services and is very similar to the one followed the world over, the only difference being that the rank of Senior Colonel can be equated to that of a Brigadier in the Indian army. The terms of engagement and methodology of promotion for soldiers make very interesting reading. All male citizens who reach the age of 18 are eligible for conscription and remain eligible till they reach the age of 22 years. Enlistment may be delayed due to a number of reasons, ranging from being the only bread-winner in the family to being engaged in further studies or having been identified by the state as possessing the potential to engage in other important activities of the state. The lowest tier of soldiers is conscripts who compulsorily serve for two years. Promising conscripts are then retained and offered varying terms as Non Commissioned Officers and

---

56   Senior Col. Chen Zhou, 'Expert Deciphers White Paper on National Defence', *Peoples Daily* 13 December 2002.
57   Richard A Bizinger, *A Paper Tiger No More*, 2003.

complemented by 'proficient citizens' with professional skills who join as NCOs. NCOs are divided into two categories, specialised technical and non-specialized technical. Interestingly, they are offered six terms, each one longer than the previous one. The first two terms are three years each with the last term being nine years or longer. This clearly indicates that performance appraisal even at NCO level is stringent and continued service is not taken for granted. Interestingly, no mention has been made of women officers and it is surprising that women NCOs are offered only one term of three years.

Reserve Services and Resettlement

A streamlined and time-tested policy for Reserve Forces has been in place for over two decades. Reserve officers are chosen mainly from officer and civil cadres who have been discharged from active service and complemented by graduates from non military institutions of higher learning and are categorized on the basis of their being assigned or not to active forces. The state actively involves itself in the resettlement of officers and civilians discharged from active service. Officers who have completed 18 years of service are given the flexibility of searching for a job themselves or being assigned one by the state, while officers with less than 18 years are assigned jobs by the state via a Unified Plan. The discharge is accompanied with a tax-free pension for life. Officers are actively encouraged to go into the hinterland and settle in their native regions as part of a 'nation building and unifying policy' started by Mao decades ago.

Mobilisation and Training of Reserve Forces

With the imminent downsizing of the People's Liberation Army (PLA), defence mobilization and the training of the reserve forces has assumed great importance. The paper attaches great importance to the concept of converting 'national defence economic potential into national defence capabilities' and shifting the economy rapidly from a peacetime state to a wartime state. This has been ensured through a three-tier management system at the central, provincial and prefect levels, which is now completely digitized. With the rapid urbanization of China, the catastrophic consequences of air raids on its cities have been well understood. Pointers from history dating back to the damage caused to London during the Battle of Britain, to Leipzig, Berlin and Dresden during the 'Strategic Bombing' offensive, and the destruction caused over Hiroshima and Nagasaki seem to have been used by the Chinese as a template for laying so much emphasis on a Civil Air Defence and rescue organization. The civil population has been completely sensitized to the procedures for evacuation and an integrated volunteer-based Civil Air Defence system is in place.

India would do well to take a cue from the People's Republic of China (PRC) considering the rapid urbanization of the country and the near absence of any kind of meaningful civil air defence procedures or organization. Infrastructure and communications have been developed with a dual aim, as alluded to earlier in the paper. The first is to build a platform for the smooth implementation of Revolution in Military Affairs (RMA) with Chinese characteristics. The second is for speedy mobilization and conversion of economic capability into defence capability. In 2003 China's mileage of railways and highways was 73,000 km and 1,809,800 km respectively, with a predicted growth rate of 15-20 per cent annually for the next 10 years. Chinese workers are annually adding about 1,500 km of routes and in the next decade China will overtake Russia as the world's second largest railway network after the US.

Militia Force Building

In order to win a people's war under high-tech conditions, the militia force is considered to be an important component. The militia is essentially an armed and trained organization comprising masses not released from their regular work and trained by the PLA to perform military duties of varied kinds, including regimental duties. This force is now over 10 million strong and primary militia members between the ages of 18 and 22 receive 30-40 days of military training every year. The urban militia is being exposed to anti-terrorist operations, keeping in mind the vulnerability of cities to terrorist attacks.

Science, Technology and Industry for National Defence

Keeping in mind the sensitive nature of research developments in defence-related and dual purpose technologies, the White Paper has only superficially dealt with the subject. It talks about "Striving to raise capability for weaponry, optimization and upgradation and flexibility of the military industrial structure and exploration of frontier technologies". Interestingly, it talks about "vigorous development of dual purpose technologies and combining military and civilian needs". Just as Indian PSUs like BEL and HAL, which primarily relied on defence orders during earlier years to survive have now diversified, Chinese military industrial enterprises have been urged to compete, appraise, supervise and motivate. This signifies a marked change from earlier years as well as a realisation of global realties. Nuclear power is being harnessed for civilian and dual-purpose use and comprised 2.3 per cent of the total power production in 2003.The Chinese nuclear electric power generation is more than 6000 MW, double India's production of 3000 MW. This capacity is expected to double by 2008 and is expected to touch 50,000 MW by 2030.[58] Having launched various application satellites, including meteorological satellites into SSO (Sun Synchronous Orbit) and GEO (Geosynchronous Orbit), the next step, though not articulated in the paper, is likely to be the launch of dedicated military satellites for ELINT, RECCE and targeting purposes.

Armed Forces and the People

Over the years, the PLA has assigned great importance to the concept of 'Identification with the People'. The slogan 'The PLA belongs to the people' is implemented both in letter and spirit. It has been ensured that the common people respect the PLA and give them preferential treatment in all spheres of life. This is termed as social preferential treatment and includes rehabilitation of de-mobilized, retired and discharged officers and soldiers along with subsidized and preferential treatment for families of servicemen in education, housing and medical treatment. Special courts have been set up to look into grievances of servicemen and local government officials have been tasked to protect property and families of servicemen on active duty. Keeping officers and soldiers motivated and respected is bound to be perceived by the PLA as a major challenge for the future, considering the explosion in the Chinese economy and the lopsided distribution of wealth. Everyone in the PLA is obliged to devote a minimum of eight days in a year to national construction and the prime activities include construction of key projects, geological prospecting, highway construction and providing special services like geographic survey, meteorological forecasting, forest fire prevention and groundwater exploitation. The involvement of the PLA in disaster-relief operations is similar to that of the Indian armed forces and needs little amplification. In the light of the increased involvement in internal security duties by the Indian armed forces, a look at the code of conduct in relation to the masses in worth mentioning. Six of the eight points for attention as articulated by Mao more than 50 years ago are highlighted below:

---

58   Raja Mohan C, 'Nuclear Power, China Races Ahead', *Indian Express* Online Edition, 18 November 2005.

- Speak politely
- Pay for what you buy
- Return everything you borrow
- Pay for anything you damage
- Do not hit or swear at people
- Do not damage crops.

Additionally, in keeping with the times and focusing on the advent of materialism and image building, the PLA has exhorted its personnel to conform to standards of bearing and turnout. Respect of ethnic and religious minorities and varied customs also indicates a realisation of the changing times. 'Unity in Diversity' is a slogan that is catching on fast with the PLA.

International Security Cooperation

After RMA, the International Security Cooperation covers the widest canvass in the White Paper, indicating the willingness of the Chinese to initiate a debate on a wide range of global security issues. It also indicates a new-found 'strategic confidence' and the eagerness to assume an 'alternative leadership' role to fill the vacuum caused by the demise of the Soviet Union. The desire for 'international legitimacy' is very evident, with a continuing reference to the 'Panchsheel' or the Five Principles of Peaceful Coexistence and the UN Charter.

Strategic and Regional Partnerships

In consonance with its focus on energy resources, strategic points and strategic dominance, consultation and dialogue has been initiated with countries that share the PRC's views on the emergence of the US as the sole superpower and the prime custodian of global energy resources. China has a strategic relationship with Cuba and Venezuela in the Americas. It has a strong presence in Africa, specially in energy and mineral-rich countries like Sudan, Angola and Mozambique. It has forged a strong relationship with the Republic of South Africa, mainly because of its strong defence industry that could provide it with cutting edge technology along with Israel. Moving closer to Asia, the PRC has an established security relationship with North Korea, Myanmar and Pakistan, apart from a stake in Iran's defiance of the US. The Shanghai Cooperation Organization, of which India has been included as an observer, is slowly but surely emerging as a significant voice in the region. This again would be effectively used to checkmate US ambitions in the 'fragmented Central Asian space', a move that has serious implications on the ability of the US to watch over strategic energy resources in the Persian Gulf region. China's relationship with members of the ASEAN has not been discussed as its strength in the region is a foregone conclusion. Taiwan and Japan remain important to China but not so much in the Indian perspective, hence them have not been discussed in the analysis.

Arms Control, Disarmament and Non Proliferation

Having firmly established itself as a legitimate nuclear power for over three decades, Chinese articulation on 'matters nuclear' reflects a desire to seriously influence global disarmament. At the same time, it justifies its continued nuclear weapon programme as one of 'strategic deterrence'. The paper clearly mentions China's commitment to the destruction of WMDs, global disarmament and non proliferation. A caveat on the issue of WMDs clearly alludes to US intervention in Iraq by stating that due cognizance also needs to be taken of the social and economic root causes of such threats. The PRC has formally joined the Nuclear Suppliers' Group and has applied for accession to the MTCR, despite being under the scanner for allegedly helping the nuclear weapons programmes of North Korea and Iran, either directly or indirectly. China is strongly in favour of greater UN involvement in the non-proliferation and disarmament debates. As the US is way ahead in the 'Star Wars' programme, it is also pressing hard for an international moratorium on an arms race in outer space.

India-Centric Summary

In the past seven years, China has produced four White Papers on Defence (1998, 2000, 2002 and 2004), indicating a stability and congruity of strategic thought between the political and military leadership. The direct and unambiguous tone of the papers indicates a proactive strategic confidence emerging out of China as against its reactive posture in earlier years. This could be a result of the strength of the economy and its emerging leveraging power, something that India also needs to exploit considering its growing economic clout. Not giving offence to Beijing has been integral to New Delhi's foreign policy posture, given its weaker bargaining position and global profile. All indicators should point to a reappraisal of this policy.

China has never aped the West blindly, a fact confirmed by a selective adoption of RMA with a 'Chinese flavour'. While China has adopted a 'bottom–up approach' by readying its force with education, streamlining human resources,

training, logistics integration and infrastructure development before introducing technology, the Indian RMA has distinctly, seen a 'top–down approach' with compromises being made in HRD and infrastructural development. It is important to understand that by focusing on the US, all other perceived threats in the future are taken care of. It is on this count that India does not find any mention in the paper. This must not lull the Indian strategic community into slumber vis-à-vis China. Despite having excellent trade relations with the US and the largest immigrant community in the US, China has the 'strategic guts' to point to the US as its primary threat over the next few decades . India too must understand that it has to focus on China and not so much on our Western neighbours, without feeling apologetic.[59] That is what 'real politik' and national interest is all about.

Just as two main leaders — Nelson Mandela and Thabo Mbeki — were responsible for the South African White Paper on defence, Jiang Zemin and Hujintao, two forward-looking, technologically-oriented, yet 'hardcore' communists, could be said to be responsible for the progress in Chinese military strategy. There is no dearth of strategic brilliance in India; it is just that the synergy and common goals are missing.

The search for energy resources has already pitted India against China in Kazakhstan and Angola, where India has lost out because of superior

59   Ganguly Swagato, 'Raising the Stakes', *Times of India,* 12 December 2005.

leveraging and lobbying by the Chinese. In the race for Angolan oil blocks, it is the promise of defence supplies and cooperation that tilted the balance in favour of the Chinese. Such is the focus of all the instruments of Chinese national interest and power, something that India has to do to ensure subsequent success in the face of Chinese competition. Both India and China are emerging out of the closet in terms of engaging other nations in joint military exercises. Any opportunity to exercise with the Chinese must be taken as an opportunity to get to know them better as long-term rivals as well as partners in maintaining peace and stability in the region. State involvement in the resettlement and rehabilitation of servicemen has to be stepped up in India to exploit their potential to the maximum. Policies have been articulated but implementation has been slow. Leaving the rehabilitation and resettlement to market forces is not a step in the right direction. Development of dual-use technologies and closer participation of the private sector in defence production and procurement, either as independent entities or in partnership with existing public sector firms, is vital to promote speedy conversion of a peacetime economy to a wartime one.

Conclusion

While it is important to make an immediate analysis of any significant document like a White Paper originating out of China to spread awareness, any meaningful analysis should fructify only after ascertaining whether a country has been able to execute what it has articulated. The objective of this analysis has been precisely that, coming as it does a year after publication of the paper to pinpoint whether the PRC is on track to execute its stated strategic objectives. Whether it is a systematic implementation of RMA with Chinese characteristics, downsizing the PLA, expanding regional security organizations like the Shanghai Cooperation Council, stepping up military exercises within the region or aggressively pursuing its search for energy resources, the PRC is well on course to emerge as a global power to reckon with by 2010. If there is one thing that India can take away from the Chinese paper, it is that strategic clarity and confidence is the first step in becoming a global power to reckon with, a USP possessed today only by the USA and PRC.

This article was published in the Spring 2006 edition of The Trishul — the professional military journal brought out by The Defence Services Staff College at Wellington.

THE INDIAN AIR FORCE AT 75: MANAGING TRANSFORMATION

The way ahead demands nimbleness in thought, flexibility and speed in action and magnanimity of the heart. Can we, as air warriors rise to the occasion?

Seventy-five years is a ripe age for an organisation like the Indian Air Force (IAF) to introspect and reflect on the years gone by. More often than not, the problems of the present and challenges of the future get drowned by the phenomenal achievements of the past that are showcased with pomp and pride. There can be no doubt about the spectacular transformation of the IAF over the last 75 years from a primarily tactical air force and perceived appendage of the land forces, to a truly strategic force with trans-oceanic reach, flexibility and firepower. The rate at which technology and platforms have proliferated in the IAF is staggering, to say the least. The share of the IAF in the defence budget has steadily risen and shows no signs of abating in the coming years. Technology assimilation, platform induction and capability exploitation have been exceptional. The international stature of the IAF has increased manifold over the last few years, especially during exercises with air forces of a number of countries. Can the IAF sustain this capability? Does it have the competencies to cope with the changing nature of warfare, the changing domestic and economic environment, and the upheavals in attitudes that are thrown up in the wake of these changes? What are our critical strengths and weaknesses? How do we ensure that the man behind the machine keeps pace with the ferocity of change that has hit India in recent times? Whenever in the past, comparisons have been drawn between the military and the corporate sector, the sheer size of the IAF has often prompted our leadership into believing that such comparisons are of no use at all. Today, groups like the Tatas, almost as large as the IAF, are changing with speed because that is the only way out in today's world. The IAF is poised on a potent technological platform; what remains to be seen is whether the pace of transformation is likely to overtake the most vital cog in the wheel, the man behind the machine.

As a Group Captain, the author feels that he is eminently positioned to carry out an unbiased and uncluttered analysis of what is right and what is 'not so right' with the organisation. If he has done his job in the manner that he was expected to, he would have a clear pulse of the officers and men below him, their hopes, fears, and aspirations! By virtue of his service (± 25 yrs) he is also in close touch with the senior leadership, attempting to grasp the 'big picture' and understand organisational goals and objectives. There is nobody better than this 'creature' to build a bridge between aspirations/attitudes and organisational goals and objective, and open up sustainable lines of communication that act as 'enablers' and facilitate convergence rather than divergence. That the 'winds of change, are blowing across the IAF has never been so clear as today, a fact corroborated by many changes in doctrine and policy, which have been incorporated over the past few years

It is important to carry out a sweeping analysis of the IAF at 75, and concentrate on the one pivotal component, the man behind the machine. The analysis would also attempt to chart a rough path for the future that may have short-term hiccups, but end up with sustainable long-term benefits. The analysis draws its essence from personal interaction with 'Air Warriors' across the spectrum of ages and ranks spread over the past 10 years.

Most of the strengths of the IAF revolve around platform exploitation, technology assimilation and tactical ability. No other air force operates such varied platforms of varying vintage and origin with such efficiency. Platforms have been exploited well beyond their expected life, albeit with a few classic hiccups; examples over the years have been the Canberra, MiG-21 and MiG-25. Technology assimilation has been so good that many of our pilots, engineering officers and men would have worked on 2–3 operational aircraft in a span of about 10 years, something that Western air forces would shudder doing. Relative simplicity of systems allowed rapid shifting of manpower from one fleet to another to tide over shortages, leading to a commonly accepted tag of a force with good crisis management capabilility.

Over the years, IAF officers and men have been valiant, courageous, dedicated and visibly made the nation proud of them. Waziristan, Kohima, Srinagar, Leh, Longewala, and Kargil echo with the valiant deeds of our air warriors in khakhi and blue. In recent times, the performance of our frontline squadrons in international exercises been praiseworthy to say the least and dozens of countries want to exercise with the IAF. Our logistics supply chain system is now 'near' world class and almost ready to support 'extended operational area capability'. There is a lot to cheer about and at the same time, there is also a need to play the devil's advocate, identify weaknesses and suggest remedial action for change. Herein lies the key to quick assimilation of technologies and conversion into capability.

Identifying weaknesses in any organisation is probably the hardest thing to do because these can be highly subjective and relative. A weakness or aberration for one generation can be an improvement for an earlier generation. This inter generational clash is, many a time, the main reason for the slow pace of change in organisations and institutions like the armed forces. Amplifying this further with some typical examples would put things in the correct perspective. The first example is an operational issue. Despite realising the payoffs and potential of medium-level attacks with both precision and non precision weapons more than 15 years ago, we waited for Kosovo and Iraqi freedom before embracing it whole-heartedly. One of the main reasons for this and one that would be hotly debated is an entire generation's fixation with 'lay down attacks' and 'hugging the deck' as being the best means of survival and attack effectiveness. The next issue is maintenance related. The induction of the Jaguar and Mirage-2000 in the late 1970s and 1980s heralded the entry of the LRU concept and second-generation Western maintenance philosophy into the IAF. Stringent criticism of the cannibalisation and 'Christmas Tree' philosophy followed the induction. It has taken us over 20 years to accept that it was time to change. What inhibited that change? Was it a belief that what worked with MiG-21s, Hunters or Canberras would work with modern-generation aircraft? Was it an archaic logistic chain that prevented speedy flow and visibility of spares that caused widespread cannibalisation or was it a mindset? It was, in fact, a generational divide and a reluctance to change with times. Nothing exemplifies our resistance for change more than an experience narrated again and again by Air Chief Marshal Tyagi, the former Chief of Air Staff. Needing a pair of flying boots while undergoing the Jaguar conversion in the UK in 1979, he found that his size was not available at base. It took the logistics department a few minutes to find out where it was available, and a day later he had his pair of boots; understandably the UK is a much smaller country. The point is that it has taken the IAF almost 30 years to set up such a monitoring, tracking and supply chain system (IMMOLS). From operations, maintenance and logistics, our quest for change resistance moves to human and hygiene factors. In the 1970s and the 1980s, whenever confronted with problems about accommodation, schooling and the likes, senior leadership often compared it to the days of the 'tents and bashas' and how lucky the current generation was to have shelter over their heads. Little did they realise that 20 years down the line, 'human and hygiene' factors like accommodation and schooling would be such important issues. A few years ago (2002), a Rand report that appeared on Rediff.com indicated that resistance to change and inflexibility of thought were two of the potential weaknesses of Indian military leadership. The report vanished from the website in a few days but to deny some element of truth in it is at our own peril. Therefore, the first issue of concern is Resistance and Reluctance to Change.

The next issue that impinges on almost everything that happens during peace or war is 'Environmental Isolation'. To explain this a little further; in the past, the profession of arms was an institution by itself and its practioners set benchmarks that society in general strived to emulate. This automatically gave a fillip to the warrior and motivated him to uphold the image that he had created for himself and the organisation he served. The same young officer of yesteryears is today part of senior leadership in an environment that has changed beyond recognition. Societal benchmarks now no longer look up to the Armed Forces as 'torch bearers of society'. Had this reality been grasped in time, the Armed Forces may have been able to put mechanisms in place to cope with these changing perceptions of society and help their personnel cope better. To amplify this issue further, a commentator (a retired Lieutenant General) at this year's Republic Day Parade very succinctly presented this dilemma on the air by saying that honour, izzat and pride were no longer the prime drivers for a career in the Armed Forces, and the sooner the leadership realised this, the faster would the three services be able to adapt to the realities of the present that have relegated the Armed Forces to one of the middle tier career preferences of the youth.

The last issue of concern to the IAF revolves around an excessive reliance on the 'Eighty Twenty' concept that revolves around old management and organisational behaviour principles, which state that it is an inescapable reality that 20 per cent of the work force would shoulder 80 per cent of the responsibility. The exodus of a large number of highly qualified professionals and excessive reliance on this concept has necessitated the development of multiple tiers of leadership with adequate redundancy. How ironical it is that at a time when technological redundancies in equipment are increasing, there is a corresponding reduction in 'Leadership Redundancies'. Except for elite squadrons and training establishments, can any commander honestly say that he has adequate leadership redundancy when the going gets tough? We do need to address this issue speedily to ensure that the 'Few Good Men' concept gets expanded to a 'Many Good Men' concept.

What should the underlying principles that govern the IAF's ability to 'manage change' be? We need to create, develop and nurture people and systems who can predict the fast-changing environment and the challenges it is likely to pose. We need different competencies to prepare to face the challenges headlong, systems and structures that are responsive and flexible enough to pre-empt the various pitfalls and road blocks that are bound to come along. The Mantra, therefore, has to be Predict, Prepare, Pre-empt. These are organisational imperatives for creation of 'Change responsive and adaptive structures'. These structures would be of no use if they are not accompanied by significant leadership changes that revolve around three I's, viz. the ability to Imagine,

Inspire and Innovate. To this, one needs to add an inescapable 'U' and that is Upgrade; something we are very good at and hence will not be dwelt with very extensively.

Ideas without structures are of no use and creating new structures exclusively to cope with change would take ages to get past bureaucratic hurdles. The answer, therefore, is to look at creating a Strategic Planning Group over and above the existing Directorates to look at four areas of focus. These areas are :

- Operations and doctrinal issues that relate to the changing nature of warfare
- Technology, with specific focus on Products, Processes, Innovations and Upgradations
- Human and hygiene factors
- Leadership development.

The IAF has always been good at training and preparing for conventional warfare. Its tactics and force structures are suited and responsive to traditional methods of war fighting that call for straightjacketed periods of training, and deployment prior to actual operations. A comprehensive doctrine and tactics for sub conventional warfare, and use of air power in protection of dispersed national interests are not yet in place. We need to accelerate our preparedness in diverse operations like Low Intensity Conflict Operations, Anti Naxalite Operations, coalition operations with or without UN Mandate, and Special operations like anti-hijacking and anti-terrorist ops. However, if one were still to identify the strongest of our structures, it has to be our operational, tactical and maintenance structures. As we go along, it would emerge that none of the structures highlighted can be viewed as stand-alone structures; they are strongly connected and interrelated, and need to be synergistically integrated

Our maintenance philosophy has always been fairly robust and effective. However, it has had to keep pace with the requirement of seamless integration between platforms, sensors, weapon systems, processes and infrastructure required to support the latest generation platforms. The inter se dependence of our maintenance structures on infrastructure development has never been as pronounced as it is today. A case in point is the continued induction of SU-30 at various bases, and the impending induction of AWACS. There needs to be far greater synergy between Maintenance/Technology structures and infrastructure development.

With monetary drivers being an important reason for officers and air warriors across the board to seek fresh pastures at various stages of their careers, there is an inherent danger of excessive organisational focus on the same. While it is very important that financial packages for personnel of all three services are in urgent need of upward revision, there is only a finite level to which these can be raised in the next Pay Commission. It would still be a fair assumption that corporate pay packages would still sustain at 2-3 times that of service personnel at all levels. If that is so, are we to assume that motivation levels ten years down the line are going to be the same as today? The answer is an emphatic yes, unless the service adopts a dual track approach of concurrently trying to refine its approach towards raising self-esteem and providing adequate avenues for professional recognition and growth along with significant improvements in remuneration. A twin-track approach to human and hygiene factors is the only way to go forward. Some of the areas that need to be looked at are listed below :

S. No.	Compensation & Lifestyle Related	Self-Esteem Related
(a)	Basic & subsidiary compensation	Changed assessment & AR procedures.
(b)	Housing, infrastructure & recreational facilities	Professional and progressive counselling, and mentoring procedures.
(c)	Schooling	More diverse rewards for good performance.
(d)	Resettlement opportunities	Prospects for lateral growth to avoid pyramidal congestion.
(e)	Opportunities for wives	

Human Resource Management has to be a key area that is manned by people with a 'flair for people'. Key takeaways from the environment and foreign air forces have to be factored in. If required, expertise from the corporate sector can be sought and tailored to the IAF's environments. Prof CK Prahalad, a management Professor at the University of Michigan is one of the most famous management prophets of 'change'. He has helped a number of corporates restructure effectively and could be approached to speak to the IAF's top leadership on change and assist the IAF in initiating major HR changes that would cater to future challenges.

In earlier days, leadership development and team building were considered as part of the HR function. Its importance has grown in recent times to such an extent that it is now seen in the corporate world as being a significant 'Force Multiplier' and driver of survival and growth. We in the armed forces have had no such dilemmas as leadership has always been seen as the 'key' to success on the battlefield. Where we need to keep pace is in 'Peacetime Leadership' that prepares soldiers for war in a relatively stable and economically prosperous global environment. We need to understand that traditional military leadership traits like courage, decision-making ability, intuition and discipline have to be reinforced, and supplemented by soft leadership skills such as team building, communication skills, conflict management skills, change management, empathy and mentoring ability. These skills must revolve around a key set of core ethics and values that must form the DNA of our glorious service. A broad set of ethics, values and skills that would make a good contemporary leader needs to be clearly articulated and institutionalised as The Air Force Way. A representative set of ethics, values and skills for the modern air warrior are given below. Most of the conflicts arising in our service revolves around Human and Hygiene factors with traces of professional dissatisfaction causing conflict too. Therefore, the issue of conflict management needs to be tackled hand-in-glove with human and hygiene factors.

ETHICS, VALUES AND SKILLS FOR TOMORROW

SKILLS & VALUES	CORE ETHICS	SKILLS & VALUES
PROFESSIONAL EXCELLENCE SELF-CONFIDENCE MULTI-SKILLING FLEXIBILTY & DECISION MAKING	INTEGRITY LOYALTY COURAGE JUSTICE RESPECT	TECHNOLOGY ORIENTATION INTELLECTUAL ABILITY

Change is a continuous process and laying down rigid recommendations violates the principle of flexibility, hence, a set of recommendations are not necessary. In fact, they are obvious at every stage of the article. To manage Transformation, Change and Conflict, we have to display nimbleness in thought, flexibility and speed in action and magnanimity of the heart. The mantra we need to follow in the years ahead must be TO STAY AHEAD AND STAY HUMAN. Air Chief Marshal F H Major, in his inaugural media address has clearly indicated that the 'human being' is probably the most important element of the IAF. We need to take this forward with vigour and sincerity.